About the Author

A Tunisian girl, Maissa is an X-ray technician, and has studied and worked for three years in Tunisia. Recently, she moved to Germany to work there. Despite her technical background, she has always had a passion for writing.

The Survivor

Maissa Sayah

The Survivor

Olympia Publishers
London

www.olympiapublishers.com
OLYMPIA PAPERBACK EDITION

Copyright © Maissa Sayah 2024

The right of Maissa Sayah to be identified as author of this work has been asserted in accordance with sections 77 and 78 of the Copyright, Designs and Patents Act 1988.

All Rights Reserved

No reproduction, copy or transmission of this publication may be made without written permission.
No paragraph of this publication may be reproduced, copied or transmitted save with the written permission of the publisher, or in accordance with the provisions of the Copyright Act 1956 (as amended).

Any person who commits any unauthorised act in relation to this publication may be liable to criminal prosecution and civil claims for damage.

A CIP catalogue record for this title is available from the British Library.

ISBN: 978-1-80439-887-6

This is a work of fiction. Some references to historical events, real people, or real places are used fictitiously. Other names, characters, places and events are products of the author's imagination, and any resemblance to actual events, places or persons, living or dead, is purely coincidental.

First Published in 2024

Olympia Publishers
Tallis House
2 Tallis Street
London
EC4Y 0AB

Printed in Great Britain

Dedication

I would like to dedicate this work to all the refuges out there who are fighting their way to a normal life, and to all who are affected by war over something called politics. This work doesn't belong to me, but to all who are waking up every day missing their home, the lost family and, more importantly, the normal life… the peace. This is not a work dedicated to a certain group or religion, it is dedicated to all humans.

Acknowledgements

I consider myself to be very lucky to have been raised by loving parents. So, as it goes, thank you, Mom, for being the best friend, the mother and the sister. Thank you, Dad, for pushing and believing in me; this work would have not made it if it wasn't for your encouragement. I am thankful to my two brothers for their excitement. My friends: Hazem, Nidhal, Kadhem, Jihen, Jihed, Wafa, Insaf, Alia, Athar, Nada, Nahla, Hassen and Moussa, you guys mean the world to me, and to the one who chose to leave, I'd like to thank you, because you have always been part of this. Sirine, you may have chosen a different path, where we are cast away, but still you should be thanked for everything you did for me, every hug and gesture. A big thanks to my colleagues in Germany who helped me through everything. The best for the end; here it is to my partner in crime, best friend, soulmate and sister, NADA, I could write about just thanking you, what you did and still do is amazing. Thank you for being there, thank you for your hard work and your encouragement, your name should be written next to me here because you were there every minute through it, giving feedback. Thank you to everyone who has been part of this beautiful journey called life.

"Why should we surrender, when we can fight?"

Every story has a beginning and so does my story... it all started with the war... That damned war!

We were a happy family, living normally. Like any other sixteen-year-old girl, I love music, movies and books, especially romantic ones. I've had my own fantasy about my dream guy, the one who'd come and take me, but please not on a horse, I want him to take me on a bike.

I've never really liked to write, I was more of a reader, but here I'm writing my own story. Well, going through hell makes you want to write not because you like it, but the sorrows and hardships you went through should be revealed to people so that you could be a kind of a hope for those who went through the same shit. Simply, you want them to pity you.

My life was close to perfection, I had many friends and a new-born brother, my father was a teacher and my mother a housewife, I've had many dreams, so I was living a normal, calm life like any other person in my age... Until that day.

It all started with the revolution, we all the Arab thought this is it, we are FREE. Everyone was up for the fight, they wanted freedom more than anything else. They wanted the right to choose whomever they want in order to rule the country, they wanted the right to speak, to criticize when they want to, they didn't want someone standing in front of their mouths and shutting them up whenever they wanted to speak.

We, the humans, are known for our great power of hiding our true feelings and building an ocean of misery inside of us. No one had the courage to show it all and fight for what he believes... until someone, somewhere, somehow put all his courage on and started the flame... and that's how it all began.

In Tunisia, it all started with a man firing himself up and every Arab nation with him.

Well, surprisingly, none of the elder ones had the guts to demand anything. You see, even when we were young, they always told us to shut it and never speak ill of the 'government'. "They'd torture you, rape you and kill you," they said.

Yet, even though they put the fear in our hearts, we didn't follow it, we always knew something was wrong, so it took a bunch of sacrifices to start the flames and even in Syria, the teenagers were the ones who made the sacrifice.

We are proud to say that we are the generation of freedom. They call us dumbass for creating a mess, I call us heroes for freeing everyone out of the prison, for waking the world up and demanding our most precious right.

"FREEDOM!"

We watched on TV what they wanted us to see, but we saw the truth on the Internet. A group of teenagers painting a revolutionary slogan on a school wall, they were arrested and tortured. Flames rose all over the country, taking revenge for these poor souls, people came out, demanding the resignation of the so-called 'president', protesters were everywhere old and young, yet the government didn't hold back and they fought badly. They arrested, injured and killed... they were merciless. A thirteen-year-old boy whose name I still vividly remember,

"Hamza Ali al-Khateeb", was arrested during a protest and his dead, bruised body was delivered to his family. They had tortured him, a boy at his age who did nothing but stand next to his brothers in the fight for his country, and yet they killed him brutally. They showed him that this world is not made for pure souls like him.

We thought one day this will all end and we will raise the flag of freedom, like it did in Tunisia and Egypt, yet nothing seemed to be ending soon and we saw the fight turning into civil wars. People were against people and when the flames wouldn't die, we attracted power countries' attention and suddenly everyone was inside and fighting for something with someone we weren't even a part of. Well, they say they were trying to fight the ISIS, but in the end, we were the victims, and none of their people died, we were the only ones dying.

Everyone committed war crimes, everyone tried to win, they used everything from airstrikes to chemical weapons, they destroyed everything we have, our homes, schools, hospitals, everyone was guilty... We won't forget nor forgive.

Back then, we didn't know much about the ISIS. Just like everybody else, we knew they were terrorists who tried to conquer the world and that we should be against them even though they are Muslims. We didn't care much about them, we thought they weren't strong enough for the fight... we should have cared.

My family and I were living in a small village in the countryside, our little town never had the guts to get out and fight like all other places did, we were like ostriches hiding our heads from fear in the sand. The elder ones were terrified and they told us to stay quiet and hide for the time being.

My father was an old activist back in his college, he told

me all about his marches and fights and where they'd hide, he even once was arrested and got his ass kicked. Strangely, he was never sad or scared of these times, he told me they were the most precious times of his life. He'd always say, "I was alive, I was fighting for something."

When the revolution first started, my dad was up to the moon, he was so happy and all his old friends called him and told him to come and fight like old days. They said, "This shit is real, they are doing something we couldn't do back then." Of course, my dad was up for the fight, but my mother wasn't. She told him that if he went there, it would be the end of everything, that he should forget we ever existed. She told him, "I gave up my study for you, you should make your sacrifice as well," and so he did, he wasn't ready to let us go.

I've never seen him so disappointed, I told him we should protest, at least here, but he refused. In this world, we always give up something for something else. I thought I would never be like my dad, I wouldn't give up my passion for anything, but I was wrong. I haven't had a family of my own yet to decide; he had a wife, a daughter and a son to protect. I heard him one day thanking my mum for stopping him. He told her, he would've made a big mistake if he went and if something ever happened to his family because of him, he would never forgive himself.

School stopped for a while, even though nothing was happening in our town, but nearby towns were literally on fire. After a while and when everything wasn't ending, our schools re-opened. They believed we shouldn't end our future.

A lot of the families didn't send their children… my father believed that I should go back to studying and he as well would go back to teach. "We should continue our path at least," he said, but, of course, my mother wasn't happy and yet that didn't change anything. We went anyway, we were both very stubborn.

One day, I woke up at the sound of a big explosion. We were already very used to that, and it was like an alarm sound.

The only good thing our town made us do was to go to school. My mum was anxious and we would hear the same words every day, "Don't go, things are getting worse, you'll die." And in the end, we would still go.

I was riding my bike as usual and my dad was riding his next to me, but things weren't as beautiful as they used to be. We had an amazing nature, big green fields filled with flowers and yet nothing that day seemed to show any signs of beauty; it's like the soul of the place was gone. Well, it wasn't odd at all, Syria's soul was gone anyway, they raped it and left it to death.

On the route, my dad stopped to say hello to his friend, and I didn't wait for him. I continued since it was almost school time and I didn't want to be late.

As I was getting nearer to the school, strangely there weren't many people standing in front. We were a girls-only school so, of course, it would be weird not to find a bunch of girls standing in front of the gate.

My mind that day didn't work like it did before, I didn't suspect anything. I just chose to believe that maybe I was too late, maybe they were already in class, so I hurried.

I used to believe that calmness is the key to live, that we should avoid the loud places and rather stick to the calm ones. Unlike people, I feared the storm not the silence. I was wrong, I should have feared the silence, I should have left the moment I heard nothing, I should have gone home.

As I was about to enter the school, I heard noises of girls screaming. At first, I thought, *Oh, they are playing in there*, but the voices weren't telling me that the person letting them out is happy and having fun. But that didn't stop me from going and knowing what was going on. I rushed to see what was happening. My friends were in danger and my mind couldn't think much, the voice inside was telling me to hurry and help, when it should have said, *Run for your life...* That doesn't mean I didn't want to help them, but I wouldn't have killed so many souls because of me.

When I arrived at the scene, all I saw was something like a war scene: one shooting a gun, another defending, one other running, girls sobbing and screaming. I didn't even have time to think about what was going on. Someone had already grabbed me, covered my head with a black plastic bag and everything turned dark. I tried to fight him, I told him to let me go, but of course nothing worked. I didn't even understand what was going on. And in the middle of the thousand noises around there, I could distinguish one voice that was screaming my name. It was dad, I heard him calling my name. I tried to answer, I wanted to go to him, I wanted to tell him I was scared, come and take me. In fact, I did scream, I did call for him, but they kept telling me to shut up. I heard him telling them, "Where are you taking her. Please, leave my daughter alone. Take me instead, KILL ME INSTEAD."

These words are still ringing in my ears. No one heard us or felt a tiny bit of guilt. They dragged me like an animal and put me in the van and my dad's voice vanished because of all the girls screaming, but one of the screaming voices seemed so familiar and I knew who it was. It was my friend Fatima saying, "Ayat, where are you? Did they take you as well?" She was crying.

I was in the deepest of despair, I thought if they are taking me, then my dad wouldn't let them. He would fight them and they would fight back, they had guns, they'd kill him. I didn't even think of what was going to happen to me, my father was in danger. I started screaming and telling the girls to shut up and I called for him over and over, but he didn't respond. I kept calling and calling with no answer. The voice inside my head kept saying, *He is gone, lose hope,* and the hope in my heart said, *Keep calling, he'll answer.* However, we all know that the heart is always the one at fault.

As the van started to drive away, I started to die inside.

All I kept thinking of was my father telling me that morning on the ride that I'm the bravest heart in our family and he is proud of me and he couldn't ask for a more perfect girl. He told me, "One day, Ayat, you are gonna make a difference in the world, I have faith in you. Your time isn't here yet, but one day, one day, my dear, it will come and I'll be there to hug you." He kept telling me that 'cause he knew I was furious that no one revolted in our town, I wanted to get out on the marches and scream for freedom. My heart sank as my mind kept believing that he was gone, he was really gone and my mind started blaming him for telling me that he would be there to hug me in my success. I wanted to scream and say, who would hug me now?

They didn't only take me, they took my dad's soul with me as well.

Chapter 1

How am I supposed to live on, to act like nothing happened? They killed my father, they murdered him. If I had the choice, I'd blow this van up with all the people inside it. They killed my dad, aren't they human? I keep asking myself why our dear God would let such animals keep living among us and destroying our hopes and dreams and taking our souls away.

Should I just throw myself out of the window? Can I do that? I don't see anything though. Can I beg them to just ease me from my pain, to let me join my father on his way to heaven? Will they let me?

And then the picture of my terrified mother and crying brother bumped into my head. *They must be so scared, they must be so lonely, I need to get back to them, to hold them in my arms and cry over the dead body of my father together.*

At that moment, I was so surprised at how my brain worked so fast and made its way out of the grief and the shock. My heart was on a silent mode but my brain kept vibrating and thinking, all the cells in my body were telling me to wake up. *You are not supposed to die, your father sacrificed his life for you, you have no right to demand death. You have to get back to your family. Yes, you still have a family left and they are waiting for you to come back.*

The conversation inside my head kept on getting louder and louder, it wouldn't quiet down. But in the end, I surrendered to the force of the brain and said, *Yes, I should do that. But how do*

I? They are much stronger than me, how will I run away from them, how will I see my family again?

The van kept going and going, and the road never seemed to end. We were stuffed like animals one beside the other... we could only hear the sound of our beating hearts, each was scared to death inside and wanted to scream her heart out, but no one had the guts to 'cause we knew we'd be dead the moment our voices reached them.

It's scary to be left inside your darkest thoughts all alone, but they say the brightest ideas come out of the darkest places.

It's hard to believe that on that particular road, I had already healed my broken heart and woken my brain to plan our runaway.

First, I needed to follow them, I needed to obey them 'cause fighting them wouldn't get me anywhere. Sometimes, we need to hold hands with the enemy in order to get where we want.

"Put all your beliefs and principals aside, Ayat. You need to be one of them, you need their trust so you can escape from them, you need to stand side by side with the enemy." I was my own calmer, I kept telling myself, "Don't you worry, my dear, bright days will come, the sun will shine again in your dark land, and you will reunite with your dear ones, the storm will pass."

Suddenly, the van stopped and there was a deathly silence. They opened the door and behind the dark plastic covering my head, I could see a little light trying to enter my darkness. Someone grabbed and took me by the hand, there was a lot of noise. Finally, the girls were awakened from their shocked states and realised that they were really taken, they weren't dreaming or imagining. This shit was real, so, of course, everyone started screaming and the men were screaming at them as well and hitting them. I could hear some of them being thrown down and getting smashed. I wanted to help them, but I could barely save myself. I wasn't like the others, I stayed quiet and followed the one who was taking me. I heard him telling me, "You are doing okay by remaining silent. You see, nothing will change if they scream, they will stay here either way and never go back home. This is your home now and you need to obey the men in here in order to stay alive. Don't think about your life any more, all you need to think about now is how to satisfy us, so we can protect you and provide you with food and shelter."

Understood, I thought.

So, basically, we were just surrogate mothers, I guess. I understood everything, we were brought here to make community, they needed someone to clear their shit, cook their food and satisfy their desires. So, what is better than a bunch of a fresh, beautiful, virgin, young teenagers to do that?

He told me to stay still, so I did. I could still hear noises and gunshots, and I heard some man telling them, "The woman who screams, kill her, she is no good. Don't they know woman screaming is prohibited? We don't need her in our community." So, they did kill a few and others were silenced.

They took off the dark thing they had put on top of my head. I could feel the sun, but I could barely see, and then my vision came back to normal. I saw a bunch of men standing in front of us and we were brought to our knees.

Their leader was standing in the centre; I could definitely tell he was their leader. He was a big man with a built-up body that didn't quite match his age. He had a long, dark beard with some grey hair in it. He looked like he was about to kill everyone beside him. I couldn't understand the anger that fills their hearts, even though they are doing something they believe in. Good or bad, it's their dream, their ambition, but I never saw one of them smiling or being normal. Even if they won a fight, nothing changed in their expressions. There was something about them... they weren't doing this because they wanted to, I guess. I could sense the fear in them, someone was scared of someone else, and someone was doing something for someone... In the end, no one actually believed in the cause.

The man stood tall and confident, he introduced himself as the leader of this community and the future ruler of Syria, inshallah.

He said, "Don't you fear us, we didn't bring you here to kill or rape you and throw you away. We are Muslims, jihadis. We don't rape. We brought you here for a good cause. You were chosen by God and you should be thankful that God brought you to us. We are the ones who will guarantee your way up to heaven. Obey us and you shall be in heaven, inshallah. Our main goal is to build a community, to bring children and raise them with our Islamic principles. We want to create a clean generation, not the ones we see now, astaghfirullah. They are letting their girls do whatever they want. Freedom, they call it; I call it the way to hell. They shall burn in hell! You are not here to fight or enter wars or even get hurt, we will provide you with protection, food and shelter. You are responsible only for your family, your chores and raising a good-mannered generation. Each one of you will be chosen by a man from our community and you will get married. You are being chosen. Women here have no right to choose who they want, they only accept what they get with a big heart... and the one who refuses to do her chores perfectly, and doesn't obey her husband, will be treated as a cheater and will be stoned to death. Let me calm you here and say we don't have to reach that point. If you behave well, you will be rewarded, inshallah. This is all in your favour. We have rules here, I am not going to tell you everything. My dear wife is responsible for this, you will be trained for a couple of days before you will be chosen by a man to marry. You could be a third or fourth or even first wife... that depends anyway. So, as I said, my first wife and the leader of the women here will be your teacher to be a good wife and mother. I won't be speaking about many of the rules, but the women all must wear niqab and when you are married, only your husband is allowed to see your face. If someone else does see your face even by fault, you will be killed. I am tired, I won't speak much more. Take them to the room, and I will see you in the ceremony, inshallah. My dears, don't you dare scream or run away and I don't like those who rebel, so I won't forgive you. That's it."

I never wanted to kill someone before, I didn't know what that felt like, but I wanted to tear that man's lips apart and pull his head out of his body! I guess that's what wanting to kill feels like. I'm not evil for feeling that; he wasn't a human, after all, he was the devil himself. I could see his eyes burning with evilness.

They took us to a big room with multiple beds, our training centre. The sun was going down and darkness took its place. All the girls were crying, and I was the only one who kept staring at the ceiling, without a single tear falling out or sensed fear coming out of my eyes. I heard one the girls saying, "Is she happy to be here? What is she, is she a monster? Why isn't she even scared?"

The other answered her by introducing me and telling her I

was a strong person even at school. "She's a weirdo, I never understood her or liked her."

My friend Fatima screamed at them and told them to shut up. She then sat right next to me, trying to talk and make me cry with her, but nothing worked on me. I was in the outer world, I was diving inside my head and making it work every cell in there to draw the plan of our escape.

Fatima told me that it is the end for us, we are captured. I turned and told her, "This is not the end, at least not for me. This is only the beginning, and I am gonna run away." Even the kind-hearted Fatima was scared of me at that moment. I guess my inner evil just popped out. Fatima was my friend, but not my best friend; the only best friend I had was my father. The girls at school liked me and wanted to hear me speak. I guess I was different and I was speaking about things they never heard of or even imagined, but I guess I was too much for them. No one wanted to get too near, they sensed danger when they got closer.

My dad always told me that people aren't afraid of me. They want to be me, they just don't have the courage to do so and that's why they don't want to be close to me, because they don't want to be reminded of their unfulfilled dreams. So, I never took their actions to heart and it didn't matter to me if they liked me or not, I liked myself enough.

I admit I was different. Even at school, all the girls wore hijab, I was the only one without it and everybody would look at me weirdly when I passed by. Our relatives always made fun of my parents for not making me wear hijab and they always told them I was impolite and I'll probably make my parents enter the hell for not raising me well. I still don't understand the wellness they are talking about; do we know for sure that they are raising their children well? Nobody knows if what they are doing is good or bad, but what I do know for sure is that obligating someone to do something they don't want to do is not a good way to raise your children. Eventually, they are going to leave and throw all of the forced principles aside. However, the principles that my family put in me will never leave 'cause they were put with love and freedom, because I was convinced by them. I am proud to say that I was freely raised, not good 'cause we don't know what good is, but at least I am sure that they put something kind and powerful inside and nothing will take that away.

I am free, a human being should be free, but they are keeping us locked in here. If I acted like I normally act, I would have screamed at that man and refused all his rules, and that's what everybody expected of me, but I am smarter than that. If I had done that, I would have been already shot and dead like the other girls who tried to speak before. I should be calmer in order to get what I want. I was as quiet as the night, but it was a chaos inside.

The night never seemed to end. The other girls did fall asleep, but I was the only one up. I just couldn't close my eyes and dive in my dreams. Even though I wanted to sleep and wake up in my house and realise that it was all a bad nightmare, but I knew that wasn't going to happen. So, I refused to approach darkness and I remained up till the morning, diving deep into my thoughts.

As the sun was just intending to rise, a woman entered our room and screamed at us. All the girls woke up scared, no one knew who she was or what was happening.

She was a pretty old woman, let's say in her late sixties.

But she seemed quite young for her age and had an outstanding beauty, which is not a very odd thing since all the women here were being chosen carefully so that the men could enjoy a beautiful view. She stood tall, she spoke openly and confidently like she owned the place, so I concluded that she was the wife of the leader. We were flattered with her presence yesterday as he introduced her, but of course we wouldn't know if it was her for sure because we didn't know what her face looked like as she was wearing niqab. My mind at that moment kept thinking that I should get close to her because I knew for sure that she is the controller of the leader behind the scenes, so her mind and words did matter and they had to be taken seriously.

I stood tall and I didn't even raise my head, showing her signs of respect.

She said, "Up, you foolish girls, a good wife needs to be the first one to wake up in order to prepare food and clean everything before her husband wakes up. We are nothing but servants to them, that's what you need to understand very well. You need to cherish your husband as if he is part of you. In fact, we used to kill the wife if the husband died in a war, but now we don't do that any more, because we believe that women need to exist in order to take care of the men and make children, in order for our community to grow. Up, I said, everyone, stand tall. We don't eat here until the men are full. Each wife now is busily preparing the breakfast for her husband. As for me, there are other wives so I am not concerned, and I have other things I'm responsible for, my dear husband assigned them to me, like training you. You are allowed to eat now, and you must finish exactly in fifteen minutes. We have lots to do."

The women came with some food to us. We ate in a hurry and then they walked us behind the leader's wife, well, everyone called her 'mother'.

We entered something like a bath. She stood and told us, "I'm not going to repeat myself much. No woman here is allowed to speak, especially in front of men. She speaks only when she's told to speak, and when one of you enters the meeting rooms of the men, don't interfere or say any word, just do what you were supposed to do and get out quietly. Try not to remember anything you heard or saw. I am here to help you become a better person, a good wife and a well-educated mother. First, we're going to examine you, we need to make sure you don't bring any illness to our precious men, and we need to make sure you are virgins. So, for those who are found to be ill and their illness could be passed easily will be shot dead immediately, for others whose illness is not so contagious will be led to do other jobs like cleaning the shit of animals and taking care of them and she would stay there right beside them and, of course, she doesn't have the right to marry. As for the astaghfirullah not virgin ones, of course with no doubt they would be killed. We don't let anything *haram* in here. The women here must be pure, like fresh water with no fault."

The examination started, we were all naked and the mother turned and examined each one of us, and telling every girl what she should do, like you have a small ass, you need to get it bigger and other stuff I don't think you would like to hear. Let me tell you that in there were all sorts of women who worked before, there were doctors, lawyers, nurses, engineers.

So, there was a doctor who did all sorts of examinations on us from blood analysing to seeing our vaginas and confirming if we were virgins or not. Everybody was busy doing something. There were like twenty nurses with more than six doctors; of course, all women and I assumed they had the laboratory equipment. It was like being in a hospital. They were quite organised so the first thing they did was to check our virginity and they would divide us into two teams. I assumed that we were sorted by who was virgin and who wasn't. They took the blood test for my team, but they didn't for the other. And why would they bother, they were dead anyway.

The girls on the other team were ten. They were very anxious. Strangely, they wanted to be tested as well because they knew this silence wouldn't lead to a beautiful ending.

After finishing, we were given niqab, which we had to wear. After everyone was covered and only the eyes were to be seen, multiple men entered. Mother called the ten girls' names and made them stand aside. They made us watch them die, as a kind of a lesson for us. We saw blood drooling everywhere.

We were speechless, we saw them getting killed so easily and we couldn't even move a finger or scream.

The mother spoke and said, "They weren't virgin, they were bad for our community. How could we make our men marry whores like them? You are pure, you haven't been touched before, you should be proud of that. But take this as a lesson for you, anyone who does not obey the rules will be killed brutally and without mercy."

I had so many objections to what she said and yet I spoke no word.

In the next days, the analysis results were out and another girl was killed; she had a contagious sickness and three others were thrown next to the animals in the corral, and we were the chosen ones, as she said. We spent the next days learning how to cook, how to take care of children, how to clean, how to speak, how to breathe, how not to laugh only in the presence of your husband and more importantly the things we needed to do to satisfy our husband's desires.

I accepted all their rules and learned what they needed me to learn and acted like I liked and believed in their principles and with days going on, the mother became fond of me and she told the other girls to behave like me and that I was a perfect example. One day, she approached me and said, "I like you, Ayat, and I think you will be a perfect mother and wife."

I thanked her and told her that I aspired to be like her, so of course she liked me even more. I discovered that I have a thing with words, I know how to speak and act and make people believe what I want, I was even scared of myself and how much I was into character.

She told me that men here are so different from each other and there are good and bad ones and that I was a beautiful girl so a lot of them would want me and that she'd help me get the better husband. I told her that it didn't matter to me, she knew what is best for me and I am sure her choice would be the right one and that I didn't have the right to demand the kind of man I want. She was very impressed with these fake words that came out of my own mouth, even I was astonished by what I said.

The training was finally over and as the ceremony day was nearing, the mother came and delivered another speech. She sure liked to speak and act like she owned the place.

On the D-Day, we spent the whole morning bathing and getting prepared.

I found it weird that they were preparing us to be pretty and presentable and they didn't make us wear niqab, so I figured that we were going to be put on display today, as the men needed to see what they were buying first.

I expected it to be an open auction, but no, it was kind of

private. There were a bunch of girls who went before me and then I was called with Fatima and another girl. The room was led by mother, her husband and three other men.

I figured out that even with men, there was a kind of priority in how they were chosen. They had grades, which classified them, like in the military, so each one had his own position in the community and of course there were ones above or under the others. Obviously, the ones in higher positions got to choose first. We were told that the men sitting there were a big deal in the community and that we were lucky to be presented to them.

They were a family: a father and two sons. It turned out later that he was the leader of the forces in the community and his sons worked with him in providing the weapons and training the men.

The father spoke and showed signs of interest in a girl called Imen. She was standing right next to me. He said as I recall vividly, "I have to make the sacrifice and choose the ugly one so that my sons can enjoy the beautiful ones. I have already tasted a lot of kinds so I am not that hungry any more."

I still remember her face, she wanted to cry out loud, yet only her tears were running down without a noise... It was a disgusting way of speaking, yet the crowd seemed to think it was a very funny joke and they were laughing hysterically. However, the younger son didn't seem like he agreed by refusing to laugh along. Weirdly enough, I sensed something coming out of him, I could definitely see the fire in his eyes.

The mother spoke and said that I was the best in the group, and the elder brother agreed and said that I was the most beautiful one he'd seen so far, and he should marry me. My heart sank as I heard him speak. He was the worst kind, he was unbearable, and he had an animal look in him. Suddenly, the younger brother stood and said that he wanted me. His brother was shocked as he was so much into me, but the father and the leader seemed to like the younger brother and respect him even more. After hours of fighting in which he didn't interfere, they concluded that I should marry the younger one. Nobody asked my opinion about the matter or who did I like better. You see, my opinion didn't matter nor did the other girls' opinions. The old man took Imen and Fatima was abandoned forcefully to the other brother, who seemed to disagree with everything and left the room with fire coming out of his head.

Everybody seemed to be happy, the purchase was successfully done, but the younger brother wasn't happy, even though he wanted me.

The collective wedding finally ended. It was a simple ceremony with no songs nor dances, just raise your hands, so that your owner could use you under the word 'halal'. Each one of us was locked in a room with a stranger she knew nothing about, a man called her husband.

I never imagined that I would get married this way, not in a million years, and yet here I was, crying my eyes out. He didn't say a word to me, and I couldn't speak as well. I was sitting like a calm, polite girl, trying to make him think that I was okay with all of this… but he didn't seem to buy it, I didn't know that back then, that he saw right through me.

I was sitting on the edge of the bed, waiting for my sentence, like a criminal giving up. To my surprise, he just slept on the floor and the only word he said was 'Goodnight'. He didn't even dare to come near me. I was in shock at first, I didn't quite believe he was different, I assumed that he was playing some kind of a game with me, so I stayed up for few hours waiting for any movements and yet nothing happened, neither that night nor the other nights. He was different, his vibe was different... he didn't belong there. Later that night, I had a very deep sleep. It was the first time I could sleep there. I guess I felt protected with him by my side. At that moment, I wasn't able to tell what my feelings were, I wasn't even ready to explain them or to believe that I could have feelings in that place. Well, I guess we will know later.

We spent days being in the same room, yet no one spoke a word to the other, we were like strangers. I'd give him his dinner and that's all, I didn't even dine next to him, each one of us diving in their own world. The weird thing was that he always said good things about me in front of the elders, even the mother was so proud of me, and his father adored me so much since I acted like an angel in front of him. But in the end, no one knew what was going on behind closed doors. We humans are very clever, we show people only what we want them to believe, and we bury the truth deep inside. I was always against that idea, I'd even get angry at my mother when I would hear her telling people other than the truth about what was going on in our family. I understand her now.

I deserved an Oscar for the acting I did, I wondered if God would ever forgive me for all the lies I told and the fake actions I did. Well, I had a purpose.

There was one person who wasn't that happy about our marriage, and he wasn't satisfied about his marriage either. His brother married my friend Fatima and since she was so innocent, of course she wasn't able to satisfy him as he wished. So, he had to do other things. He consistently complained about her and he even married another and treated her like shit. Fatima was so nice and she couldn't bear that kind of treatment.

I told her to wait and I'll let her out of there, and she'd always say, "I may not be as brave as you, Ayat, but I promise you that I am going to make it out of here, one way or another."

I used to be happy hearing her speak like that, but little did I know that her way out was by killing herself. Fatima did win, she did leave before me. She was braver and stronger. When I heard about her death, darkness hugged me again like a lost friend and hope fled away. They didn't even bury her, since suicide is prohibited in our religion. They threw her in the forest, for the animals to kill her.

That night, I waited for everyone to go to sleep, including my husband, to go and say goodbye to her one last time.

As time passed by, I had memorised the entire place and known all their tricks and guards, so I was able to make it into the forest. Fatima wasn't my close friend, but she was a human after all, and every human being deserve to be buried at least.

I wasn't even scared; I knew I could be dead in a minute and yet nothing mattered to me. When I arrived, I saw her pure body being eaten by a bunch of wolves and I couldn't even bear to look. I had to think fast and quick, how to make them go away. They are not a bunch of cats you could just scream at. Suddenly, I heard a gunshot, and the wolves ran away. I thought that was the end of me, they had found out and now I was dead. I o pened my eyes and accepted my destiny, and I said to someone I couldn't even recognize, "You are going to kill me anyway, so please make it quick. I do not regret anything. I am sorry, Fatima, I wasn't able to protect you but I am going to lay next to you, my friend. We shall go there hand in hand… together."

That someone said coldly, "Stop talking nonsense, I am not going to kill my own wife. Let's bury her quickly, before someone sees us."

I felt something inside my stomach, it wasn't pain for sure, I hadn't even eaten that night, but it was something kind of beautiful, I guess. *Is this what they call butterflies?* I had to wake up, so I hurried to him. He started digging the ground and then we put her inside and he told me to stand behind so we could pray for her.

We did everything we could for Fatima, may her soul rest in peace.

As we walked back home (I hate to call it that), I was walking right behind him, my face facing the ground and him in front of me, not speaking but telling me to be careful of the stones every now and then. I surely was expecting a kind of punishment or some big talk, but no, he was silent the whole time.

It was very dark, so one of the men guarding the place came near us, screaming and asking us where we had been. My husband stepped ahead and looked at him with such piercing eyes that even I was afraid of them. When the man recognised his face, he immediately backed off and even apologised.

We entered the room and still he didn't say a word, so of course my burning soul couldn't bear that. I said, "Why would you kill me with your silence? Just say anything, blame me for going out, tell me why were you there and why did you do that even though it's against all your rules and principals? Speak, man, say anything... don't keep me standing here, assuming stories and diving in my thoughts with fear."

He was so calm even though I yelled at him, and then he said, "There you go, I knew you weren't as calm as you acted. I felt your fire from the first time I laid my eyes on you, I saw your burning soul wanting to speak back to our boss on that first day, and yes, I did fall in love at first sight with those burning eyes. You looked so smart. Believe it or not, Ayat, I am not what you think I am. I am not here by choice, I am a hostage just like you. I don't usually smile here, but I did when I first saw you. Yes, I do love you and I won't kill you and I will help you do whatever your mind spends days on thinking, there is no one here that means to me as much as you, you are the only person I care about in here now."

I was speechless, neither my mind nor my heart could've accepted that. How could I be loved? *Someone like me can be loved?* Well, I couldn't be loved, not in there… but I was loved deeply and honestly.

After a moment of processing all of that, the thoughts came rushing into my head and my heart was saying a totally different thing. It was a battle inside, but how could I dare to have a battle that way, in there, in that situation? How could I possibly be having feelings for the enemy? I could have said a lot of things at that moment, but I chose silence and I needed peace to think, so I didn't say anything and went to bed immediately, and he didn't even demand a word back from me.

From that day on, everything changed between us. He'd speak to me and he would tell me everything about what has been going on. He'd tell me secrets that shouldn't be known to anyone about the community, like their future plans, attacks and where they hid the weapons. I was anxious and wondered why the hell was he telling me something like that. It was as if he was helping me figure out what should I do in order to run away.

I was and still am a person with a very strong personality, so I don't stand things being not clear or taking hints from each other without speaking face to face and that's why one day, I chose confrontation and I faced him by saying, "I am wondering, why would you tell me all of this? I am well aware that men in here shouldn't be telling their wives about the secrets of the attacks and the whereabout of the weapons. As you already know, we exist here to serve you only, we aren't allowed to use our brain or even think, and here you are telling me overnight everything and even taking my opinion on things. I think I have the right to know why are you behaving like this."

He answered as calmly as usual. "I think you already know the answer to your question, but you choose to ignore it." He had a playful smile on his face, which made me even angrier, so I yelled at him.

"I am not buying those words and even if it's true and you are in love with me, this doesn't make your actions understandable."

The smile left his face as he was speaking, and his eyes turned serious.

"I respect you, you need to understand that, and I respect your brain and I know you are capable of so many things, yet you are imprisoned in here. I am just trying to refresh your brain by talking to you and trying to save him from fading away."

I don't know what happened to me that night, but I kept on pushing our conversation out of the line and kept trying to make him angrier and speak his mind, so I answered in a ridiculous tone. "Very good, still not buying it."

He had it with me, so in the end the smile turned to a scream. He shouted at my face like he never did before. "I AM HELPING YOU! AREN'T YOU TRYING TO RUN AWAY?"

I wasn't even shocked, I knew he knew. "Yes, I knew, but I needed to hear it from you and why are you trying to throw all your beliefs and community aside… to put yourself in danger, to disappoint your father. Just for love?"

He answered, "Even though I insist on my words and one day I'll prove to you my sincere feelings by actions, but I have other reasons. I have a story behind it and the things they believe in… I don't. They don't represent me, and I am not one of them after all."

Of course, I had many questions, but I just asked a general one. "What do you mean by that?"

That night, we didn't sleep, I wanted to hear an explanation of all his words, so Adam started telling me his story. Oh, I never told you his name, right! His name was Adam, the saviour Adam.

They lived normally, none of them knew that one day everything would change. They were a family of four, he described his mother as the most innocent soul. His father never showed any signs of belonging to some kind of a community, but in fact, he was preparing to form one with other people without even telling his family. One day, he told them everything and forced them to go with him. Of course, his mother refused to let her boys live such a life and be surrounded by this type of people. She told him to go and do whatever he wanted and leave them alone, but he didn't. Adam was only four years old when he witnessed the death of his mother by the hands of his own father, right before his eyes.

The elder son was already so attached to his father and he'd do everything he asked. Adam, however, was taken away without understanding anything, he was just a kid. He told me, "I am punishing myself by staying here, my mother was killed in front of me and I stood there watching without moving a finger, without trying to save her…" To live without love is hard enough, but to live with the guilt is even harder. He blamed himself for something he had no control over.

I kept looking at his eyes the whole night. How can someone survive this, how can someone live after this? I found it quite strong and quite weak at the same time. I wanted to protect him and be protected by him. He ended the story by telling me that he would do anything to protect me.

"I can't see someone I love getting killed again," he said.

Our daily life changed after that night. We'd spend the day apart, since he had to work, and I tried to act as the perfect wife in front of others and in the night, we'd plan my getaway.

But there was someone who was planning our destruction. You guessed that right; yes, his own brother. He was so jealous of our relationship and how his father liked me as well, so one night, he called Adam out and then he entered our room and I wasn't even wearing my hijab. I told him that Adam wasn't here and that he was the one who told him to come out to meet him.

He told me, "I am going to give you a choice; either you have sex with me right now and no one will hear about it, or I am going to say to everyone in here that we did it together and you already know the result of that. No harm will come to me. Come on, Ayat, my wife is dead, you need to console me. Wasn't she your friend?"

Of course, I refused. He didn't even try to rape me since he knew I'd scream and no good would come to him from it, so he went out furious and after a while, Adam came back and he told me that he couldn't find his brother and he kept searching for him. I couldn't keep it to myself and told him everything. His reaction was weird, he told me that he expected that from him, since his brother was a selfish man and he kept saying from the beginning that he wanted me as his wife, so he felt betrayed when Adam married me. He told me not to worry and to leave it to him.

The next morning, there was an announcement saying that everyone should be gathered in the big hall. I knew it was related somehow to us and I felt that my death was near, so I left a letter telling Adam everything I wanted to tell him and I told him to run away and go find my family for me. If I couldn't finish this myself, at least he could do it for me and he was the only one I could trust with this.

The leader took the centre of the place and stood firmly, all signs of his body saying that something terrible was about to happen. He said that someone was going to die today, because they did something we as a community could not accept. At that moment, I was only thinking about Adam. I tried searching the hall with my eyes for him and yet there was no trace of his existence there. I wanted to hug him and say goodbye one last time.

His brother came forward and put an act of guilt and sadness in the eyes and said, "Yes, I did something with one of the women in here, since I was so sad that my first wife killed herself. But I felt the guilt afterwards and I wanted to tell everything. I can't keep hiding this any more. I had sex with my brother's wife and she accepted it with an open heart, without refusing anything. I am to be blamed but she is the one who seduced me."

Everyone looked at me with a murderous eye. They were ready to blame everything on me and I had no right even to stand up and speak for myself, so I stood silent. Adam and his father just entered the hall and he stood with immense anger coming out of him. He spoke for the first time in his life before them.

"I believe that my wife is innocent and that my brother is doing this because he is jealous of us and he wanted her for himself. I trust my beloved wife and I believe that everyone in here can witness how devoted and good she is. I am not going to say much, I am just going to demand one thing; I love my wife so much and I didn't want to make her feel obligated to do anything against her will, and since she is so young and pure, we didn't do anything together. Logically, she'll still be a virgin, but if she did have a physical relationship with my brother as he claims, she'll no longer be virgin then. Therefore, I demand our doctor to examine her and declare the truth. Of course, it will happen in the presence of our mother so nothing could be fabricated."

I didn't say a word; I was so proud of him. The leader accepted his request gladly and I went to be examined and, of course, I was declared innocent. Adam's father was ashamed of his son's doings and therefore he suggested to the leader that his son should be punished for his immature actions.

That day, everyone apologized to me, and they even liked me more, but the thing is, all the men and even women made fun of Adam for not touching me, and they were telling each other that he wasn't 'strong' enough. He did prove his love to me, because he put his pride as a man on the edge. Even his father wasn't happy by his declaration, and he sent the mother to me in order to know the reason behind that. I told the mother that there is nothing wrong with Adam, he only respected me. I told her that I wasn't ready, and I was scared, so of course she gave me a whole lecture about why I should give myself to him and that it is wrong to let him wait like that. I kept pretending that I heard her, but in fact my mind was wandering in a totally different place and time.

That scene keeps visiting my imagination until now, I still remember the look on Adam's face when he was defending me. Back then, I didn't know the meaning behind all of this, I didn't quite believe that someone would put his life in danger to save the one he loves. But now, I know that is very normal; when a man falls in love, he doesn't fall only for the body and the eyes, he falls for the soul.

I heard your thoughts, just now. You thought my life would turn suddenly into a romantic movie, didn't you? But no, let me disappoint you and say we did love each other, and more than Noah and Allie loved each other in *The Notebook*, but we had a bigger problem than our families disapproving of our love.

We spent days planning my escape. There was no future or family talk between us, I wanted to open the discussion and make him leave with me, but I delayed it for a while, until the plan was ready.

There was one car that was allowed to come near our camp, and the one who drove it wasn't from the community. He was a gun dealer, he brought arms and ammunition to the place, so that car was my way out.

Since Adam was the one in charge of getting the weapons, he was already very close to that man. So, what we had to do was to give this guy a little money and he would accept our offer gladly, because as Adam said, that man would do anything to get more money and that's what he did. Adam had already set up everything with him, without telling me much of the details. He said that the little I knew, the more safe I would be. So, I just followed him blindly through this plan. My trust was something very rare to be given to someone, I don't even have a best friend who had my little secrets with her, but strangely or not so strangely, I gave my full trust to Adam. Well, it was not just a little trust, it was more than that, I entrusted him with my life, and he did deserve that.

Everybody put their faith and trust in me, they said I fitted right in their community, and that I was going to be something very big in the future and they would give me big roles, but little did they know, I was the most unfit there.

The days seemed to run by slowly, but as the day of my planned escape came closer, the excitement started to fade away and the fear started to grow bigger. I know I should've been happy, but I just couldn't be, since I was leaving Adam and I wouldn't be able to see him again and I was sure he was not going to be happy being left alone in there. So, I made a vow to myself that I was going to take him away with me. He was already my husband and my mum would definitely love him because he reminded me so much of my dad.

I sat down at dinner and I put the delayed discussion into action. "Adam, I don't want to leave alone, I want to take you with me. I don't think I could live without you in my life." His eyes gazed at me and then he smiled a sad, yet meaningful smile and said playfully, "So, you're telling me that you are in love with me, right?"

I didn't answer that because I was so shy and my cheeks were so red and hot, I thought I had a fever. Well, excuse me, I've never been in love before. And then he spoke seriously. "I can't live without you too, and I will be more than glad to leave with you and we can start a whole new life together, but I just can't leave. They will go crazy, they will search the whole country for me and they will kill you and me. But if you leave alone, that will be dangerous too, but much safer than the both of us leaving together. They can let go of a girl who knows nothing about their plans and secrets, but they can't let go of someone who knows too much already. To be honest, I don't have the courage to put you in that kind of danger."

I argued that we could find a solution and everything would be okay, but he couldn't be convinced. Well, neither was I. I just spoke out of pain, but I knew that it would be impossible for both of us to leave, just one is hard and risky enough.

The day finally came. That morning, I did all of my chores perfectly and then I went back home and I found Adam there. He stood in front of me, gave me money and said, "You were the best wife someone could dream of, I won't forget you. I won't love anyone else but you, I'll carry you in my heart till my death and beyond if I can. I want you to forget everything that happened here and you are allowed even to forget me as much as that hurts my heart, but I can't keep you in the past. You need to build a beautiful future for yourself and for me, I want you to make both of our dreams a reality, and never forget that you are not alone. I am always with you. The man will guide out of here sound and safe, he promised me, so follow him and take a good care of yourself."

My tears were falling out and I couldn't hold myself, I just kept telling him to leave with me, I didn't care about the risk any more, all I wanted was for him to be with me. But that man had a heart of a lion; no matter how much I cried or screamed, he wouldn't fall for any of it. In the end, I gave up, wiped my tears away, hugged him tight and for the first time I said the words he was longing to hear: "I love you" and "I'll never forget you".

I could see both the happiness and the sadness in his eyes. He just kept looking and me, the way he always used to look, and guided my way out of our little home. I never liked to call that place my home, but I came to learn that home isn't a place, it is wherever your loved ones are.

Everything went smoothly, as planned; it made me scared for a while. *It couldn't be this easy,* I kept thinking. I had a bad feeling about it, but Adam kept assuring me that everything was fine and nothing bad was going to happen. The man came and sealed the deal with Adam as usual, and Adam made me hide in the truck and put a bunch of things above me. There was a little hole I could see from and breathe through, and I still felt uneasy about it, but I had no other choice other than to lay there and wait for the truck to start moving and praying that our plan works.

As the truck started running, my tears started falling as I saw Adam getting farther and farther away. I still remember the smile he put on his face that day; it was different. It was a mix of many feelings. His tears were falling, but he forced himself to smile for me. I wish that was the last thing I saw.

I was watching him with my eyes and suddenly he fell to the ground, and as he fell, the vision got clearer and I could see the gun that shot him. My head was turning wild, I couldn't believe what I saw for a while. The vision was clear as water, but my heart wouldn't believe what it saw. I tried to get away, I tried to get back to him, but the driver started screaming at me, telling me to shut up. I tried to get out of there, but I was locked, there was nothing I could do.

The men started running after us and shooting guns, I don't remember how we got away from them. At that moment, nothing mattered to me, I couldn't think straight. I was in the outer world.

As the time passed, and we started to get further away, I started screaming even more, telling the driver to let me out. He wouldn't shut me up now, he just left me to deal with my grief, the way I chose to do it.

People fear the silence before the storm... I tend to fear the silence after the storm.

After the wildest screams and tears, I went silent, staring at the hole, hoping to see other than what I saw. Nothing changed. When I came to realise that all of it was true, all I could think about was, I was the reason Adam died.

I took his life.

Chapter 2

*"They say you can forget and move on;
I say not in a billion years."*

Close your eyes... imagine the most precious person to you getting killed. Felt the pain? Did you feel like your heart was being squeezed?

Did you feel your mind going blank? Did you feel your knees falling to the ground? That's where I was.

It wasn't enough that they took my dad away from me, they killed the only person I trusted and loved. The only person who accepted me for who I am, the only person who sacrificed his life for me.

I started screaming again, so the driver stopped and helped me get down. I started shouting like a crazy person and told him that I was going back and I was going to kill all of them. He started to calm me down, but I wouldn't, so he yelled at me, "HE DIED FOR YOU AND YOU'RE DOING THIS? STOP THE CRAZINESS! HE SACRIFICED HIS LIFE FOR YOU, YOU ARE NOT SUPPOSED TO GIVE UP NOW. GO OUT THERE EXPOSE THEM. TAKE YOUR REVENGE IN ANOTHER WAY... Don't be like them, Adam did warn me this may happen and I made him a promise, that I would protect you and get you where you are supposed to be. He told me not to stop, no matter what happens. He was my friend too, you know, and I saw him being killed, but I didn't stop, not for you, but for him... and now you need to live not for yourself, but for him."

I didn't know what to say, so I just rode in the car next to him and I told him to carry on.

The time never seemed to pass, and we weren't reaching anytime soon. The sun went down and all that was ahead of us was a dark path with no light except for the one coming out of the car. Suddenly, a bunch of guys blocked our way and the driver had to stop. They got near us and started asking questions like where are you going, who is that and more. The driver lied to them and told them I was his wife and we were at my parents' and now we were going back home.

One of the guys never seemed to move his eyes away from me and he said, "How could a beauty like you marry a bald like him?" and all of his friends laughed and he continued. "I think you deserve more than a loser like him. Come with me willingly and I'll make you reach the sky." All of them were having a blast and laughing hysterically, but I didn't seem to enjoy any of it and I remembered that before leaving, Adam gave me a gun and told me to hide it and to use it only in an extreme situation. I stepped out of the car and they were happy, they thought I was going with them. Without thinking, I just pulled the gun out and they weren't even scared, they were convinced I wouldn't kill any of them. But I was capable of doing more than that because my life wasn't only mine any more; I made a promise to reach high, so I was ready to crash everyone on my way.

That guy said, "Come on, angel, put that gun down. I know you can't do it; you are just going to hurt yourself."

I answered with a coldness I didn't know I had in me before. "Leave us alone and I won't hurt anyone; come near me and I'll kill you all."

They laughed and came near me, telling me to cut the act. I was dying inside, I knew they wouldn't leave and they would rape me and make me suffer even more. A pure soul like mine was being stolen from me and I couldn't do anything, but I was capable of doing something.

So, I shot him down, I shot a man down. I killed someone. After the gun did its job, I threw it from the shock. I saw blood everywhere. I kept thinking, *Who am I, what am I doing?* They started running after me and I started running as well. The driver drove his car toward the guys and hit them. They all fell down in a second. I got back in and we literally flee in the car.

From a normal teenager to Islamic jihadist to a murderer… I was not reaching high; I was diving down.

We both spoke no words until we reached his home deep in the forest. His children came running to him as soon as they heard the car, and his wife opened the door and welcomed me with the purest smile, and I was thinking, *Would she be welcoming me like this if she knew I was a killer?*

She put out food for me, but I ate nothing. They were like a normal family, trying to invite me into their warmth and home, but I was diving in the thoughts and guilt.

After dinner, his wife Mariem, her name was Mariem, came near me and spoke, "I know everything that happened to you, you poor soul. You are so young to be suffering this way. My dear, that's life, I am sorry you had to witness the ugliness of it so early. My dear, be grateful even for the little, small moments you had with the people you loved, there are people out there living without memories and that's even scarier."

As she spoke, I started remembering the warm hug of my mother, the jokes of my dad and the way he looked at me, my little brother and his restless energy, our neighbours, our green land and, of course, Adam and his beautiful smile...

She held my hand and said, "You are strong enough to fight. You are the light, don't let darkness take over you. You have a mission to do; you need to live for them, not for yourself."

I started crying and she hugged me tight, I cried till I felt my eyes fell down. I don't even remember how many hours I kept crying and Mariem never left my side, until I felt asleep.

The next day, I went with Ahmed, yeah, that was the driver's name. He looked like a man out of a 90s movie, but his name was pretty modern. I said goodbye to the beautiful family and held Mariem tightly in my arms, then I left. It was only one night and yet I felt like I was at home.

On the road, I had millions of questions I wanted to ask Ahmed and I took the courage to do it. "Why are you risking your life and your family's by delivering guns to the jihadis?"

He replied, "I knew you were dying to ask me that. Well, I didn't have a choice, I was a farmer like any other, but I had a lot of relationships. I made friendships with all kinds of people; the bad and the good ones, the criminal, the doctor, even the lawyers, so I guess those people saw me and knew I was perfect for the job. They kidnapped my wife and my children and threatened me if I didn't do as they said, they'd kill us. So, I was obliged to do such a shameful job. I don't think God will ever forgive me for this... I helped those bastards to kill my people, that's why I live there with my family. It's a place that no one knows about and that's why I wasn't afraid this time to help Adam, because I was leaving them anyway, I was just searching for a way."

"God knows everything and he'll surely forgive those who

deserve it. But aren't you afraid they may find you? I don't think that place is very safe any more and we even made more enemies last night.

"Of course, it's not safe any more. As we speak, my family is being taken by a friend of mine to a boat. I will go too as soon as I deliver you home and we will leave the country for good. You see, my wife is not from here, she's Egyptian and we are going there," he replied.

"That's great. I am really sorry you are sacrificing a lot of your time on me."

"No, this is something I am proud of. At least I would have done something good before I left."

The road wasn't as dangerous as I thought it would be. The police made us stop once and we said we were married, and they just let us go.

As we got nearer to my little city, I became more and more familiar with the roads, but they felt quite different.

I suddenly screamed saying, "I am home." I saw my house, and it looked the same as before, nothing had changed, nothing at all.

I thanked Ahmed and said goodbye and made him leave because his family was waiting. I didn't want to make him any more later, but he gave me a number and told me to call anytime I needed anything and that he would be more than happy to help.

It was weird. Everything was the same; the buildings, the whole neighbourhood, it was like I never left. I kept imagining my dad standing in front of the house and talking to everyone passing by, the smell of my mum's food coming out of the house and running through the whole street and the crying of my little brother. Everything seemed to be the same, yet nothing was the same.

I wanted to take a walk through the streets, to see again the places I knew too well, but I couldn't; the excitement of seeing my family ran through me and I couldn't wait to go and hug them as much as I wanted. A few hours ago, it was a faraway dream and now I could feel the reality of it nearing.

I knocked on the door and my tears were running. I was expecting my mother to come out and hold me tight, yet no one answered. I thought maybe she was at one of our neighbours'. My mind refused to think negatively about this.

So, I decided to go and look for her. As I walked past the streets, trying to find someone to ask, the town seemed to be quieter and quieter. I walked through the street searching for any living soul and there seemed to be no one there. I knocked on doors, screamed my heart out and still no one answered, and yet my heart refused to believe that they may have left.

Suddenly, a voice, a familiar voice called my name. I turned immediately and I knew the face right away. It was Aunt Aicha, our neighbour. She was an old lady and everybody loved her and respected her, she was very close to my parents as well. She didn't have children or a husband, she was a loner, she had lived alone all her life, and enjoyed every moment of it. She used to tell us all of her stories and adventures. Well, she didn't live her whole life there, she used to be a traveller. Every week in a different place, but when age hit her, she went back to her homeland in order to rest in peace. She said, "there is no other country in this world that is more beautiful than our dear Syria." Well, I don't think she found much of a peace there.

She asked with hesitation, "Is that you, Ayat? I can't believe my eyes. Is that truly you, my dear?"

I answered with more hesitation, "Yes, Aunt Aicha, it's me. Oh God, I missed you."

"We all cried tears of blood when they took you. My poor child, what did they do to you? Did they hurt you? Did they hit you?"

"Aunt, I am really fine, nothing is wrong with me."

"My dear, my poor dear," she said, crying.

"But, Aunt, where is everyone? I can't seem to find anyone in here."

"Oh, no one stayed, they all have been deported. I am the only one left. They wanted to force me to leave, but I refused. If I am going to die, I am going to die in here, in my country, not in some other place."

"My family, did they leave as well?" I asked.

"Yes, my dear, your mother left in tears, afraid that one day you will come back and not find her here. She begged me to leave with her and when I refused, she told me to wait for you and to help if you ever to come back, and here you are now standing in front of my eyes."

I was lost for a moment; I didn't know what to do or where to begin. *What am I supposed to do? How can I leave? How can I find them in this big world? They could be anywhere,* I kept thinking. But I knew one thing at that time, I had to find them, no matter what it took.

I stayed with Aunt Aicha for days, trying to think about a way to come in contact with anybody who may know where my mother and my brother were. The days seemed to pass by slowly and the fear kept tearing my heart apart. All I heard those days were the bombs and guns. Aunt Aicha really seemed to live in hell surrounded by death every day, it was more frightening than the ISIS community, and we were unprotected.

I asked her why did she put herself in danger like that. she told me, "My dear, I lived a beautiful life filled with happy moments and adventures, I have nothing to regret. I did everything, falling in and out of love, being heartbroken and breaking someone's heart, leaving and entering... I experienced everything according to the plan I made when I was young. It's true, not everything went according to it, but still most of the things I wanted came true. My plan was to live everywhere and taste everything and it ends by me settling back in my old town and dying here. I don't care if this house falls apart on the top of my head or they'd bomb me out, I just want to stay here. I always stick to my plans, I don't fear. I am a woman and women have superpowers. Once there is something they want, they stick to it until they get it and that's what I want now."

I was so proud of her and her personality and her attitude, she was a role model.

One day, Aunt Aich remembered that my mother told her that my Uncle Farid would help them settle somewhere.

I remembered that my Uncle Farid lived in the capital and he was a very well-known lawyer with a lot of connections to higher society people, but he never was there for us and he always blamed my dad for staying in the countryside, telling him that he'll never get rich as much as he did. But I had no idea what had happened to him since the war broke out. Aunt Aicha knew one of the men who helped everyone get out of there, so she called him and he didn't know where my mother may be, but he knew exactly what had happened to my Uncle Farid... To my very surprise, he had been imprisoned due to some reasons. I found it weird since my uncle was a very suck up man and he wouldn't go against the government, he had always been a very obedient 'dog' to them, getting all their dirt clean and that's why his relationship with my dad was very bad, so I thought he would be at the top by now.

I knew where he was imprisoned and the man promised to help me meet him. He told me that he wasn't one of the protestors, so it wouldn't be very hard to try and talk to him. Aunt Aicha was close to this man and she made him promise to take me there himself and to do whatever it takes to protect me, so this man had to come to us especially. If it weren't for these people, I wouldn't be alive right now.

I waved goodbye to Aunt Aicha and promised to come back to her if nothing worked for me and she told me that her home was always open for me.

I made an acquaintance with the man who took me on the road. His name was Mohamed and he was in his 30s. He had a very new kind of thinking, I had never met anyone who spoke like him before. Well, except my dad, all the boys and the men in my town were very strict and serious and they didn't like being discussed, and that's why the majority of them despised me saying I was too much and everyone kept saying to my mum that if your daughter keeps acting this way, no one would want to marry her. I want to take this chance to say, I got married and I was deeply loved for who I am, not for who you want me to be.

So Mohamed told me that my uncle was a very disgusting man and he was a shame and I couldn't agree more. He told me about his dirty work and how he'd bribe the judges to help him win the cases and how he'd help the rich ones get clean and how he'd step on the poors and he wouldn't be even sorry for it. So, I asked him if he was such a loyal fella, why was he imprisoned.

He told me that he was imprisoned just for the image. His dirty work had been published in a journal and since the higher ones were already dealing with a lot, they put him in a jail to show the people that we don't forgive anybody and we punish everyone for what they do, so he sacrificed his freedom for their image. But, of course, he wouldn't really be imprisoned that much after all, it would be more like a vacation.

Mohamed told me that he had a friend who worked at that prison, and he already arranged everything and that he told my uncle about my visit and he accepted it. Everything was going smoothly.

We arrived. I entered and sat in a room, waiting for him to come.

I hadn't seen him in years, actually, I didn't even remember how he looked like. He never visited us, and we never did as well.

He entered, smiling, and he hugged me, thanking God I was okay. He kept saying I grew up and I became beautiful and all that bullshit and I was just smiling back but not quite interested in all of this. I wanted to tell him that I came for a reason, not because I missed him. But I couldn't since I needed him to remain in the mood in order for me to get what I wanted out of him.

I said, "Uncle, I heard that you helped my mother and my brother to get out of here, so do you know where they are?"

He answered in a much deeper voice, "When the 'rebellions' first broke out, I knew things won't be as beautiful as they used to be. So, I sent my family abroad. They are living now in Turkey, but my love for money kept me from going. I decided to stay on my own because I knew what I gained here wouldn't be comparable to what I'll earn there. Well, eventually, I am good."

I said angrily, "Well, I don't care about all of this, I don't care, do you understand? I want to know where you sent my family."

He was shocked by my outburst and said, "How could you scream at your uncle? Didn't they raise you correctly? I am not going to take it to heart, I know you are in a very bad place right now, stressed and scared and all."

I was thinking that screaming won't get me much, so I calmed down and said, "Please, I don't have much time. Can you tell me now?"

"Well, when your mother asked me for help, it was too late to do anything and she wanted a better future for your brother, so I told her she had to leave the country, and she accepted. She was ready to do anything."

I tried to remain as calm as possible and asked him, "So, where did you send them?"

He spoke in an annoying tone, like in the movies when a villain is telling his story, but absolutely without any drop of guilt. "Believe me, I hadn't much of a choice and your mother didn't have enough money for the plane, so I had to send them illegally."

I couldn't stay calm any more. Well, no one could stay still after hearing him say that, so I just screamed at his face, "Do you possibly mean by a boat in the sea? You wouldn't do that! You have enough money to send everyone in here abroad, and you couldn't do that for your own brother's family? Are you even a human? Are you really his brother? I can't see the resemblance."

"Stop screaming, I have a reputation in here to keep."

"I don't care about your fucking reputation, you—you...

Okay, just tell me that you at least were sure that they arrived soundly."

"About that, I don't quite know, since I was put in the jail a day after," he told me coldly, without thinking about the circumstances of his doings.

I was angry to the point that I couldn't scream at him any more. He sent them like that, threw them away without even checking on them.

After a while of cold silence, he spoke. "I know something, but I don't think you'll want to hear it from me. I am going to give you the name of a journalist, a wild one. He was a very close friend to your dad and he'll tell you where you could start searching. That's all I could do for you and I'll appreciate it if you never visit me again. You are a very impolite girl and I hate this type of personality; it reminds me of my foolish brother and father."

I was furious, I wanted to say and do many things to that man, but I made my way out only after saying, "You are a shame to our family and God shall never forgive you for your doings."

I left carrying nothing but the name of a man who may help me. I left carrying nothing but despair and fear. I left carrying the hope of finding them.

I rode in the car with Mohamed, and we started discussing the next step. He immediately recognised the name of this journalist and said, "Amir Rahali is a very famous journalist. He is one of the bravest hearts I've ever met. He wouldn't sell his beliefs even for gold. He has his principles and he fights everyone. Since he is much hated in here and he was imprisoned for more than three years because of his article, he later left the country and settled in London, where he got his master's degree in journalism. He built a career for himself there. He wrote about everything without fear, and he was threatened with death a couple of times. He even went on an interview once and said that he'll never get married or have any children, so that he wouldn't have anything to be threatened by. He didn't want them to have any weak points. He didn't even have family; both of his parents died when he was young. When the revolution first started, he came back to Syria and fought with everybody else. He said he had to live this. Even if he was no longer young, he needed to fight for a bright future for the generation who fought for their freedom. I remember him once standing in a march and telling us that he is proud of us, that we did something they weren't courageous enough to do. Of course, when things weren't working, they wanted to get rid of him quickly, but since he was a very important person to all of us and he was the only one who could speak the truth without fear, we couldn't let him die in waste, we needed him. So, we made him go back to London secretly. Even his colleagues in London helped. He still writes articles about Syria and fights with us, but let's just say in a different and a secret way.

"I have his contact, so we will just go over to my house and try to contact him via Internet. I think I know something about your family too, but I am not sure if I am the right person to tell you. I think it'll be better if he tells you."

I said, "Why does everybody keep repeating that?" I didn't even have the strength to fight or scream or beg him to tell me any more; my energy was fading. I felt my whole body being drawn out, so I just went with everything he said without an argument.

We arrived at his home. When I entered, his mother welcomed

me with an open heart and offered me food. Well, I ate, I needed that. As we were sitting, the sounds of bombs wouldn't stop and everybody were acting normally as if it was the sound of music.

His mother noticed my astonished face and said, "Try to think of it as some kind of a music, contact the sounds together to make a beautiful melody. It will be much better that way, the fear will go away."

I tried to put it together, like she said, and there it went... a loud-sounding rock music was going inside my head. It always surprises me how people can make everything beautiful; even the most tragic moments can be turned into a beautiful memory if we want to. We humans have a brain and thanks to this organ, we have imagination and imagination is the most powerful magic that ever could exist. We could just close our eyes, open our minds and create a whole new world inside. We could get rid of all the shitty things going on right now. So, I did close my eyes and turned this rock music into some kind of a magical melody and I started imagining.

I am walking right now on the beach wearing a beautiful white dress, feeling the water in and out of my feet. The air is the purest I have ever smelled. I turn my head back and I see my family far away from me. My brother is running all around the place, my mother and father are walking hand in hand, enjoying the moment, and they stare at me with the most loveable stare and wave. So, I wave back. Just as I am about to jump in the water, I see them there, I don't want to leave, so I run back to them. I keep running and they smile from afar, waiting for me to arrive.

"Ayat." Someone said my name and woke me up from the only peace I had in a very long time. I opened my eyes and

Mohamed's mother was standing near me, saying, "Wake up, my dear, you fell asleep last night and we just moved you in here. It's morning already and Mohamed is calling for you. I think he found what you were looking for."

I wasn't fully awake, nor fully asleep. I think I lost my mind for a while; I didn't even know where I was or who was talking to me, but after a minute, the reality hit back and the pain grew tall again.

I went to Mohamed, hurrying, and he told me that he had found him. He said that he had some work to do and he'd come back to us after a few minutes. So, I just sat next to him, silently waiting.

After a while, he called back. Mohamed answered him and then he left, leaving us some privacy and then he turned to me and spoke. "Is that you, Ayat? I can barely recognise you now, you truly are just as beautiful as your father had described you. I just can't believe that I am seeing you right now. We were so worried about you, are you okay? Did they do anything to you?"

I just kept staring without saying a word, I kept staring at him, and I saw tears in his eyes, but I could feel him trying to hide them. I kept clinging to my silence, so he tried to approach me with everything he had. He kept trying to converse with me.

"Do you know, Ayat, that I was the one who named you? Me and your father were quite the best friends, we were known in the university for our everlasting friendship and loyalty to each other. We never fought, we were inseparable. We both had big beliefs and dreams, we had the world in our hands, we were fearless. He was my one and only family, after all. I was mad at him when he chose to settle; well, I can't blame him now since he brought such a beautiful soul like you to us. When he fell in love with your mother, he decided to give up on everything he believed in, in order to make her happy. He decided to live his life by her rules. I didn't respect that at first, I didn't even attend the marriage of my only best friend. That's one of the things I regret the most, but he kept calling me until I answered and he invited me to his home and I entered your beautiful, cosy home and I just understood why he'd given everything up for this. I was even very close to your mother and when they first told me about you, I felt like my own child was being brought into the world. The happiness when I first held you in my arms was unimaginable and your mother at that time turned to me and said, 'You should name her, I don't think any of us could find a better name than a journalist.' I smiled, I didn't even think for a second and I just said out loud the name 'Ayat'. You are probably wondering why you don't know me. Well, because I left your side when things started getting worse for me. I didn't want anyone using you to threaten me, I can't accept the fact that you could get hurt. So, I decided to go away and never contact you again and that's what happened. I haven't seen your family for years and it still hurts every time. When I think I couldn't even see my own best friend before he went… it still hurts."

His words sunk deep in my heart, I felt the pain inside, I felt like I wanted to hug this strange man. Well, he didn't feel strange to me, I felt like I had been by his side for a long time. I felt his sincere words and feelings.

We stared at each other and then we both started weeping like babies, screaming our hearts out for our lost family.

After a while, I came back to my senses and I asked, "Could you please tell me what everybody is trying to hide from me?"

He gathered his courage and told me, "I knew what your brother and you look like; your father sent me pictures every year. When your mother tried to leave the country, of course she didn't turn to me because she was afraid. I am a very hated person in there and I wouldn't have been much of a help to her, even though I may have been better than your stupid uncle. Anyway, I know people everywhere around the globe, that's how I collect informations about refugees. When things got worse, I tried to reach out to you, to know how you were doing, and then I got the information about your father getting killed and you being kidnapped. I did everything I could to find you but I couldn't, I guess I wasn't powerful enough, and then I tried to find your mother and brother and resources got me to your uncle and I came to know that he already did sent them away. But that didn't make me lose hope, I kept searching everywhere for them. Until one day, I was scrolling on the Internet and this picture of a little boy kept going everywhere. I had a bad feeling about it. This boy was found on one of the beaches of Turkey, dead, drowned. His face wasn't quite showing in the picture, so I called everyone I knew, and they told me they kept the body in Turkey and if I might know him, I should go there to identify him. So, I went… I won't say much, it was indeed your brother, Ayat. I am sorry he had to leave us at an early age in one of the cruellest ways."

There it went; another slap on the face. There he went; another loved one taken away, and here I was, left alone in my sorrow again. They killed him, they killed my little brother… he wasn't even capable of pronouncing his name correctly yet, why? What did he do to live in such a cruel world? Don't they have hearts, how could they throw him in the sea like that?

I didn't say a word; tears were nowhere to be found. I guess

I had predicted it. My mind went on remembering the beautiful moments I had with him, when he was running around me, when he laughed at me, when he kissed me, when he was afraid at night and would come to sleep next to me, when he'd run away from Mum and hide behind my back. My little soul was gone. I guess it was better 'cause this world isn't made for innocent souls like him.

I didn't even have the right to grieve, I had to think about my mother and if she was dead too, so I asked him in the coldest way, "Do you know anything about my mother?"

He answered, "I spent weeks searching for her. They said they found her body next to him, but thankfully they were able to rescue her. She was in a coma for a month. I stayed next to her. When she woke up, she remained silent, not speaking a word because of the shock and then when she started speaking and waking up a little, I begged her to come with me to London but she refused. She simply said that she is going to live next to her people until she dies and that she didn't think that she'd be able to live much in this world anyway, since everyone she loves are gone. So, she is currently staying with the refugees in Turkey. I spoke to her a few times and I visit her there whenever I have the chance, but it's been months since we spoke last time. She has refused to talk or even see me, she told me that I remind her of all of her loved ones and she couldn't handle it, so I left her to her freedom. She will be very happy to see you safe and sound, I'll call her immediately."

I said, "No, I want to see her face to face. Don't tell her yet. I am going to ask you a favour, can I?"

He answered with a smile on his face, "Of course, I'd give my life to you."

"Could you help me get to her? I don't think I can do it on

my own, and I believe you wouldn't like it if I went illegally."

"No, of course, don't even think about it. Just give me a few days, me and Mohamed will arrange everything to get you out and I'll even meet you there in Turkey."

We hung up, and I was set still not quite sure I was in the right state of mind. I needed to process everything and understand what was going on.

In the next few days, Mohamed and Uncle Amir used every connection they had to get me a passport and a visa so that I could travel. The process took more than three weeks and I stayed with Mohamed's family. They were very kind-hearted people and they treated me like I was one of them, a part of their family. I was the rude one, I didn't answer much when they spoke to me, I didn't do chores around the house. I didn't even smile back at them. But they understood my situation. The thing is that I wasn't alive nor dead, I was between the two. It was chaos in my head, I kept looking at my brother's picture on the Internet and I wondered how he'd felt. He had suffocated to death, he must have tried to breathe but he couldn't. My angel, how cruel is the world to show a pure soul like his the worst face of it. I hope God led him to a better place. I thought he was too pure to live in our world, the purest hearts don't deserve to live in here. The world would destroy them if they stayed. I always thought to myself, why am I still alive, I should be the one dead. This all happened because of me. If I had stayed home that day, my father wouldn't have been killed, my brother would have stayed alive and grown up... I am the only one that is to be blamed. As much as I wanted to meet my mother, I was afraid she wouldn't be happy to see me. She'd tell me I was the cause of it all. But the fear wouldn't keep me away from her; even if she hit me, I'd still go to her.

A few days passed by and I was still sitting in the same place, waiting... Mohamed came one day with my passport and visa in his hand and he told me that everything had been arranged and my plane was leaving in two days.

I didn't have many clothes or stuff to pack, but Mohamed's sister gave me some clothes and stuff that could be useful. On my way out of the house, Mohamed's mother came close to me without speaking a world, and his father came near and told me, "I am a pretty old man, I have a lot of experience in this life and still I never met someone as brave as you. I could say with a big heart that we should expect big things from you. I think you'll be one of our ways to light. Keep fighting, my dear, and always know that we have your back and don't ever say that you don't have a home in Syria. Syria will always and forever remain your home and we will welcome you back at any time, our home is always open for you."

I didn't say much back then, I just cried and hugged him and said in a low voice thank you, and that I'll never forget them. I walked out.

Mohamed drove me to the airport. On the way, I took a good look at my country. I knew I'd be back there someday, but I needed to save these pictures deep inside my head, so I could have the motivation to come back and fight again for my lost land. But the view wasn't as beautiful as it used to be; the houses were destroyed, lands were abandoned and yet I still feel the beauty deep inside of me and I know for sure that one day my Syria will regain her beauty.

I thanked Mohamed for all the things he did, and I told him to visit Aunt Aicha from time to time and to take care of her for me. We said goodbye and I left, I left my home country, I rode the plane and left, left my people, but I remember telling myself that l will be back with more power and energy.

On the way, I didn't think much, I just wanted to meet my mother, to hug her and tell her how much I missed her scent. I wanted to ask for her forgiveness; I started all of this, after all. I was the reason my father and brother died. I hoped she wouldn't hate me, I hoped she could hug me back like she used to do. I was determined to beg for her forgiveness anyway. She is my mother after all, she wouldn't leave me. I had hundreds of thoughts and millions of fears and yet the courage was filling me up. I wasn't thinking of taking any step back, I thought to myself that I am going to get my mum back and I am going to fight for my country till my last breath.

As I walked out of the plane, my heartbeats kept getting louder. The moment I walked out of the airport door, I saw Uncle Amir standing looking at me with tears in his eyes and then he got closer to me and hugged me, saying, "You made it. You worked hard and you are finally here, I am proud of you." Those words calmed my burning heart like magic.

We rode a taxi. I remember him telling me that we need to go to the bus station because the refugee place is far away from the city. So, we rode the bus, sitting next to each other. I remember Uncle Amir telling me all about the stories about him and my father, and I was so excited like a little girl. I wanted to know everything. It's like I never really knew my father. His version of my dad was much more courageous, stronger and revolutionary. He told me that they were unstoppable, nothing could hold them back. They were tortured, threatened and even once almost killed and they never backed up, they had no fears.

He told me, "I hated your father for abandoning our

principles at first and leaving me, but I was wrong. I should have never blamed him, he was in love. I kept thinking what a fool my friend is, he just got himself fears, weak points, but now as I see you sitting next to me and I see your burning eyes, my friend was smart, because he knew we needed someone much stronger than us, a generation who could turn this world upside down and you did and you will succeed. I know for sure that you are going to do all the things your father and I weren't able to do."

I said, "I promise you that I am going to fight, I am going to free us."

We kept chatting on and on, the entire road, nonstop, we were never bored of each other's stories and I kept on laughing, it was my first smile in a while. At that time, I remembered something Adam told me before.

"Don't be afraid, along the way, you are going to meet people as pure and good as you are. We are meant to meet people like us, and that's why I met you. So, always open your heart and never be afraid of being abandoned or broken, and if you ever feel that way, dive deep inside of you and you'll find me there holding your hands." I smiled as I remembered those words and I thought he was right; well, Adam was always right.

The bus stopped and Uncle Amir told me that this was the place. I stood in front of it, I saw the tents everywhere and it seemed like everyone was busy with something. As we started walking across the tents, the faces seemed familiar to me. I felt like I belonged there, I felt like these were my people, I finally felt like home.

Uncle Amir was well welcomed in there, everybody seemed to know him and welcomed him. They told him that they missed him and they thought something bad had happened to him since he had been away for so long. I came to a conclusion that he used to come there a lot and help the people and provide them with food, clothes and even shelter. As I listened to one of his conversations, I came to know that he even helped orphans to find families.

As warm as this place may look like, but the situation was still very bad. The weather was freezing, and they were wearing clothes that couldn't even cover them. Their faces were tired, they looked like someone who hasn't eaten for days, and it may be true. I heard them complaining to Uncle Amir about the lack of food, clothes and a lot of other things. He apologised for leaving them during this period without help, but as I quote exactly from them, they said, "We are not blaming you; we know that you had your own reasons. We missed you, we didn't miss your food or money." Pure hearts always remain pure.

The children were playing, not worrying about a thing. I came close to one of the girls there, and she was so beautiful with her green eyes and black hair.

I played with her a little bit, while Uncle Amir was figuring out where my mother was. We had a friendly conversation as well, she told me they left Syria when she was very young, so she doesn't remember much about our country or how it looks like, and that her dream was to visit Syria.

I took the honour of describing our country to her, I didn't tell her how things looked like right now, I told her about our true Syria, our beautiful Syria. The other kids were interested as well, so they came to listen, and everybody seemed to have a lot of questions about this subject. I could see the happiness in their eyes when I told them about our homeland. They smiled and it filled my heart with hope and happiness for the first time in a while. Even the older ones were happy to hear me speak that way about Syria, they told me you just took us for a ride back home.

We finished our conversation with laughter and I waved goodbye to them, promising that I would be back with much more than hope next time.

We started walking again, getting closer and closer to my mother.

I was busy watching what everybody was doing, the women there were cutting vegetables, the men trying to start a fire for the women to cook by and the children running from place to place, filling it with love. I bumped into Uncle Amir as he stopped suddenly. I started laughing because I was busy looking everywhere but not in front of me. He didn't react to my laughter, so I turned my eyes to him, and his face was telling me to look ahead.

I looked and there she was, my mother. She was sitting on a chair, looking ahead and not blinking an eye. She carried all the sadness inside of her. There was an old lady that came close to us and said, "You are curious about her? Well, we all are. We know nothing about her, she hasn't spoken a word to any of us since the day she came here. We think she may be, you know, a little crazy, so we don't get that close to her, so be careful."

I didn't even have the power to answer her, but Uncle Amir did that for me, and he even pulled her away. I started walking to her step by step. I stopped on the way, a big fear overwhelmed my heart, telling me, *What if she doesn't want to see you, what if she hates you, because all of this happened because of you.* I died at that moment. Uncle Amir got close to me and asked what was going on and I told him that I am not going to go to her because she must be hating me.

He held my hands and said, "There is no mother in this

world that could hate her own kid. All your mother told me back then was that she hopes you come back to her alive. At first, she was sure you were alive, she told me that her daughter is much stronger than we think and that she is going to fight her way back to her. She had faith, she waited for you, she *is* waiting for you, so stop saying this bullshit and go and hug your own mother."

His words calmed my storm inside, and I told myself that even if she hated me, I didn't care. I loved her enough for both of us, that I was going to make her forgive me.

Without any further explanation or description, it was a simple encounter, full of unspeakable words. I just stood in front of her and my eyes were filled with tears. She rose her head and told me, "You are here, Ayat, it's been a long time. Your father and brother always come to visit me, but you never did. It's okay, I am happy as long as you did come in the end. I missed you, my angel."

I just smiled, I didn't even want to ruin her moment. I sat down and touched her hand and said, "Mum, do you feel me? Do you think a dead person could be felt when they are held? Were you able to hold Dad or Malek before?"

Her eyes widened. Uncle Amir said to her, while he was standing behind me, "She is here, she is not dead, your daughter is back."

She started weeping and screaming and said, "Are you real? You are not dead? You are really my daughter Ayat?" and I answered, "Yes, it is really me, Mum."

She held me like she would never let me go, and all my fears washed away. I got my power back, I got my hope back, I got my family back.

Chapter 3

"To live is to suffer, to survive is to find some meaning in the suffering."
– Friedrich Nietzsche

They say life is unpredictable, we can't confirm anything or deny it. Sometimes, we are riding a big wave, up in the sky, and others, we're deep down, drowning in the ocean.

I never thought I'll be able to meet my mother again, to hold her deep in my arms, to feel her beating heart next to mine. I saw her, I felt her, and I still couldn't believe it was real... I kept looking into her eyes, I kept holding her hands, afraid that if I let them go, she would vanish.

Nothing changed, she was still my mother, she looked like my mother, but something felt different, she felt different. My mum wasn't always that much of a hyper person, she was rather quite rational and serious, she was always conscious with everything she did. I always questioned my dad for marrying her, I felt like they were so different, yet my father never questioned it. I remember very clearly that I was once very angry at my mother because she didn't allow me to travel to the city to attend this big protest against the government. Of course, she wouldn't allow it, I went to my dad and I told him, "Why did you have to marry such a boring person, she's nothing like you, she's different. How could you sacrifice everything for her? I really can't understand your decision."

My dad was always the calmer one; even though he was a

very active person in the past, he didn't have big reactions like I did, so he said to me, "Your mother wasn't always like this, she's nothing like the person she's trying to be. You remind me of her, you have the same energy. I know that people tell you that you act like your father, but no, you're much braver than I am, you're like her. I still remember the first time I laid my eyes on your mother, it was at a big protest in the city and girls weren't very likely to be at such events, but your mother was different. She was not only attending the protest, she was leading it as well and screaming her heart out. That was the day I fell for her and I made a vow to myself to marry her. Ayat, everybody has a story, and your mother has one. She had a best friend before, her name was Mariem. She and your mother were inseparable, they were more than sisters. They attended and led every event together, even when I wanted to get closer to your mother, I had to take Mariem's permission first and when she liked me, she allowed me to go near her. I remember Mariem telling me that if I broke your mother's heart, she would tear me apart, like literally. She always meant every word she said. Mariem was a brave activist, she stood against her family just like your mother did to fight for everything. However, one day, the big heads in the government decided to shut us, so they kidnapped Mariem, and we couldn't find her. We searched everywhere for her. Until after a few days, her body was delivered in front of your mother's house. It turned out that they raped her and threatened her to shut up, but she was braver than anyone could imagine, so she fought them until her last breath and of course they were irritated by her courage, let me say more afraid than irritated, so they killed her.

"And your mother became the person we see. She was devastated, she wouldn't leave her room for days, she blamed herself for her death, but in the end, I stepped in and I tried to save her from the darkness. I'd like to believe that I succeeded a bit, but of course she can't forget any of that, none of us can. So, when we decided to get married, she made me promise her that we will leave everything behind, because she didn't want to lose anyone any more. I made a choice, I loved her, and I never, nor will ever regret that decision. She was more important than everything."

After that day, everything changed. I started seeing my parents as heroes because they made choices and sacrifices I didn't think I could ever make.

We sat next to each other, not being able to let of our hands and Uncle Amir left us to give us some privacy. I told her everything; I told her about Adam, about my journey and how I found her.

She kept looking in my eyes and crying, she thought I had been through a lot, but she didn't know that none of that mattered to me any more, because I had found her.

I thought she hadn't fully believed my father and brother's death, but she knew everything and believed in everything that had happened, but she told me that imagining them and talking to them was the only thing that kept her alive. She was about to kill herself before I appeared, she thought I was dead too, and there was no reason for her to stay alive. But God offered her a second chance and me as well.

A second chance, a revenge. I was determined to take revenge and protect everyone, and I'll make the change that many were afraid to make.

After hours, Uncle Amir came back. He was trying to help the people there and get to know the problems and to find solutions to them. I was impressed by the way he looked; he was cool… he shined.

"So, what's next? I know that you both have already lost a lot, and I lost too, but we have to move, we have to keep living. If it's not for us, at least for them. We have to make plans and move forward with it," said Uncle Amir with ambition coming out of his eyes.

"As much as I hate to make any plans my dear husband and son are not included into, but they would be very sad if I left Ayat alone. Yeah, you are right, we need to move on," answered my mother.

"I want to change the world, I want to lead the change, and I don't think I can do it here. We need to sacrifice to achieve what we look for… I say, let's open our arms wide for the new future and accept the reality, to keep going," I said.

"Yeah, well said, Ayat, let's embrace the new us. About the sacrifices, as much as I want to take all of these people with me, but I can't, so you have to come and live with me. I am going to try to make it all work. Next to my house, there is a little studio. We could rent it for you to live in and I will ask my connections to get you a residence permit card, and Ayat needs to start her school again very soon so that she could be our hope for a better future," said Uncle Amir.

I thought my mum would be against my future, but she wasn't. I saw a spark coming out of her eyes, she was ready to fight again, she knew that being quiet and a coward wouldn't lead us to any better solution. Even if you hid in the shadows, they're going to come after you, so better stand in the light than to hide in the darkness. I want to die with dignity not with shame.

We travelled to London. We stayed at Uncle Amir's house for a bit until the studio next to him was free for us to live in. The thing you don't know about Uncle Amir is that a lot of people hate him for his honesty and the vivid image of the reality he publishes, but others admire him and his honesty. Nobody gains anything without pain. He didn't only sacrifice his personal life for his work and country, but he has also been through a lot. He didn't speak much about the past, he chose to let go of the pain so he could move forward, but he told me once that the most brutal arrest he had been through was back in Palestine. He was there as a journalist and he published a lot of articles about the brutality the Israeli government does to Palestinians. It was his duty as a journalist to tell the truth, but of course the big heads wouldn't like it that much, so they arrested and kept him for weeks. He didn't exactly tell me what they did to him, but from the tone of his voice I understood. It was beyond explanation and imagination; however, he was much stronger than them and after he had been let out, he came back and wrote even more articles about the truth of the prison of Israel. He wouldn't let me read them, he preferred to show me only the bright side of the world and he wanted me to experience the darkness on my own.

He was and still is one of the infamous heroes, he does everything in secret, and he helped refugees and took care of the homeless. Since the day I moved in near him, there wasn't a café or restaurant in my weekend, we took turns from a refugee centre to the other, trying to deliver food and clothes, trying to do whatever we could to help these people. My mum also changed, she stepped out from her hole and started doing all the charity work on her own. She built a whole new world for her, she did much more work than we could do, she knew the refugee centres and their problems better than all of us, because she experienced living there, so there wasn't someone who could do this job better than her. Her enthusiasm went far beyond our imagination. Sometimes, we couldn't even find her and she would call back and say that she went to another country for some work. She even helped and still helps Uncle Amir with his articles.

Uncle Amir always went on a field journey and he never let me go with him. He said I'll have my own journey one day, I shouldn't rush things and I shouldn't share the journey with other people. He always said that the journey of life need to be led alone. It's true that we need support from family and friends, but they would never walk it for us. This is the road you need to walk on your own, in order to get to know your true self and establish a whole new you through the hardships along the way.

So, as I said before, Uncle Amir had friends who liked him and some of them were head politicians, so basically everybody helped us to get our papers. For me, it was easy since I was still young and I needed to go to school. My mother wasn't quite that old as well, so they registered her in a university and actually it was a good plan, since she couldn't finish her diploma. My mum wanted to be a journalist and there she was, trying to be one. It was funny how she studied with people at the age of her daughter, but she didn't care, she was a new-born child with dreams.

For me, I worked my ass off. Studying among British teenagers wasn't that much of a pleasure… they treated me like trash, trying to bully me and hit me, but little did they know, I was much stronger than them. They called me a terrorist, well, they weren't quite wrong, I was a part of ISIS. I married one of them, so I guess I was pretty dangerous. I wanted to make that very clear to them, I made them fear me, so that they won't come near me and so they didn't. I played smart. It felt lonely, but at least I didn't back off trying to cry myself every night to sleep.

I am sure all of us have experienced this once in their lifetime: people around us always told us to stop dreaming, to stop hoping for things out of our reach. I've heard that quite a lot in here, even more than Syria. My friends back then always hated me for having big dreams and thinking differently than them. How could a girl think of other plans than marriage, kids and cooking? Our only joy is clothes and our happiness lies in the hands of our husbands. I was and still am different, I thought that being in a developed country would help me out of there, people would encourage me to follow my dreams. Out there, nothing is impossible, everything is possible, but little did I know that nothing changed. At least, back in Syria, they don't do actions, they only bring you down with words and arguments. But in here, they fight you with words, actions and the law if they can. The school was a game of bullying, and the bullies were heroes in it and the nerds played the role of NPCs; they exist only for the pleasure of the principal characters. I was an NPC myself, but I made myself an exception. I forced the main characters out of my sight. If the school was the game, college was the monster level of it. The bullying was even harsher, and they were unstoppable. They didn't fear or back off and no one stands by your side. Why would they care about a Muslim girl trying to reach the stars when she can't fly? They thought by treating me like that, I would back off, I would give up my dreams, my patience, but they didn't know what I've been through to get here. Their words and actions meant nothing; I was ready to kick every bullet out of my way to get there. To touch the stars as they say. In fact, I did reach the stars, the proof is that you are reading this book.

I became an advocate at the age of twenty-five; it doesn't happen a lot, actually it was a big deal, everybody talked about me: "the refugee who made it". Well, if they knew the truth, then they would have written the ISIS's girl has become a lawyer. I became a lawyer, I became a lawyer for poor people, refugees, people in need. I didn't become a lawyer to make money or protect the big heads in the governments in order for them to play dirty freely and I am supposed to clean the shit they make. I fought the injustice and am still doing it, being threatened to death hundreds of times, but I am standing still. I learned to protect myself and the people surrounding me. Because my death will mean the end of the war and they don't get to decide that. We are the one who will decide when the war will be over, and we are not considering 'the give up' method, we are going to fight until our last soul. So basically, the war can only be over when we win.

I tried to be involved in everything. At first, I played it safe and I stayed with the big lawyers companies. Of course, they hired me not because I was the top of my university or brilliant, but because I was famous and everybody wanted me because they wanted the attention and I needed them to understand the industry and to collect information in order to protect things in the future and that actually worked. After that, I started my voluntary work with the help of Uncle Amir and Mum. We travelled the world trying to help as many people as we could. Sometimes, I travelled alone and I experienced the darkness as Uncle Amir said. I was part of the UNICEF, so I was allowed to go to a lot of places for my work. Besides, I was the lawyer of the refugee community in London.

I am not going to talk about the misery of the world that I saw, we will need a whole other book for that, but I have to talk about one of the experiences that will never be erased from my memory. Uncle Amir said that I shouldn't ever forget it.

I was interested in the Palestinian case as much as any other Arab person and very active in it; it was a matter of pride for us. Uncle Amir had great and bad memories there and even my mother went there multiple times as a journalist. (Oh, I didn't tell you that my mother became a journalist, and she works in the same newspaper as Uncle Amir since he is the head editor now and they are doing great work together.) So, they always told me about the beauty of Palestine and how things were there. I was curious and I thought I could definitely help. At that time, the 'Israeli government' and the Palestinian citizens were in a bad conflict over a certain case, so I decided to go there to help and see how things were in reality.

My father always told me about Palestine, and I was and still am a big fan of Ghassan Kanafani. For those who doesn't know him, he is a Palestinian writer and a warrior as I would like to call him, so I was very excited to go there, to experience and see the things that Ghassan had written in his novels. It was my father's dream to go to Palestine, he dreamt of it since he was young, he had a vision, he had a cause and he had a case to protect, so I carried that dream deep inside and promised to make it happen not only for him but also for us.

Everyone kept talking about the beauty of Palestine and the feelings you got the moment you stepped on its ground. Well, they weren't wrong about it; the moment you enter Jerusalem, you are hugged by this feeling of warmth and the people there are out of this world. I can't even describe how nice they are.

Everybody welcomed me there as if I was a long-lost cousin. Some of them did recognise me and said that I was doing a great deal for humanity, especially Arabs and others. Of course, and other didn't, but that didn't stop them from inviting me to eat in their houses.

I liked it there so much, it felt like home. It felt like I was back in Syria, I felt like I belonged there and did try to help them as much as I could. I stayed for months there, kept travelling from one place to the other, getting to know the truth behind the polished media, and make long-lasting friendships. You know, they say sometimes you go on a life-changing journey, and the 'you' who left first is not the same you that comes back days later, and I did experience that. I wouldn't say I changed completely, but there have been a couple of changes there. My view of the world did take another turn.

I believe I did a lot of things for the community back then and I opened their minds to a whole new different prospect. We were ready for the war, but not with guns or grenades. We were preparing our minds and knowledge for it and that of course made some 'Israelis' angry and they couldn't stand it when someone angers them, so they took me in. The Palestinians tried to protect me, but poor souls, they didn't have an authority to help me and, of course, I couldn't let anybody sacrifice their lives for me, not any more.

So, I went with them quietly, trying not to run away and not to make a big fuss out of it. I was locked in their prison for disturbing the general opinion of the citizens, which is not even a crime, but that's okay, it's a crime to them. I stayed there for a month. They didn't use the extreme punishment on me, like sexual harassment, taking off the clothes, being locked away, and so many more, because they knew I couldn't stay there forever and I didn't seem like the type of person who'd shut their mouth when they are out and of course they couldn't kill me since I was a very known member of the UNICEF, so they just kept me there. Sometimes, when I argued with them by complaining about the way they treat the other prisoners, they fought back by not giving me food or water for days, or the handsome men in the army would come and show themselves 'naked' to me. I shouldn't explain that further and I am not even able to repeat the words they told me back then. They seemed very good at speaking both Arabic and English, so the words were very varied, but, all of that meant nothing to me. What mattered to me the most was every night I'd hear screams coming out from other cells. I didn't only hear, I saw things too and I wasn't even able to protect the other person. I know I shouldn't be telling facts and reality because there are people who don't like to hear it, but I am here to tell the truth; we are not living in a fairy-tale, this is the real world and we need to face the reality in order to save what we can save. In the cell in front of me, there was a fifteen-year-old girl. She was so beautiful and nice, she always called me in the night and told me that everything will be all right and that the moment we got out of there, she is going to take me with her home to meet her family and make me taste her mother's food. She used to tell me that her mother was the best chef in the world. We used to stay all night talking and reminiscing about our countries and families, I even told her about my little brother and Adam and she loved both of them. She told me that she wishes to marry someone like Adam in the future and I used to tell her that good hearts always find the hearts like them and that she would definitely marry an even better man than Adam. She had the most beautiful smile in the world, she always laughed, she was very optimistic about the future and she told me that it didn't matter to her even if she died, because we all exist to protect and love Palestine, so if they had anything more precious than their souls, they would have sacrificed it for Palestine. The people there didn't like how bright she was, but they liked her face and body, so one day they came in a pair. As they started raping her one after the other, I was asleep at the time and I woke up on the screams of her, calling my name and telling me to save her. Of course, I screamed, cried, hit, yet nothing worked. I watched her with my own eyes being ripped apart. I saw her innocent soul being taken away and I wasn't able to save her. I still blame myself for what happened to her. I know back in the time, there wasn't much that I could do to save her, but still the guilt exists. After they finished their job, they left her lying on the ground. I kept calling her name, but only her eyes answered with pain. The tears kept falling down and not even an inch in her body was moving. I kept begging for help, but no one came. At the end of the day when she fell unconscious and her eyes closed, they came to take her to the hospital. Days and weeks passed, I kept asking about her, but no one answered. They told me I was imagining things and that there was no one in the cell in front of me. I was not crazy or imagining, she was as real as the sun. Even after I went out, I kept looking for her, trying to find any clue, but till this day, nothing to be heard. I did search for her family and went there and tasted the most amazing food made by her mother, but I wasn't able to tell them the truth. I wanted only the good memory of her to keep being alive, the bad remains deep in my heart.

She wasn't the first or the last who suffers; every night, you'd hear all kinds of screams and you're just sitting there waiting for your turn to come, waiting for your death sentence.

I faced all kinds of feelings there, from guilt to weakness to sadness to depression to severe depression. That meant having the thought of killing myself because I couldn't bear to watch and hear all of that without being able to do anything. They weren't human, they were happy to treat them that way, they used to call us 'animals' there, they told us we were not human, we were not part of the human race and God made us for them so they could abuse us and our only goal in life was to amuse them. Isn't it scary to raise a whole generation based on that kind of belief? They were brainwashed, they believed in what they said with all they had and there was no place for anyone to argue or change that. You could see that in their eyes.

The UNICEF fought for me, of course. With the pressure of the people and my family, after a month 'of teaching me a lesson', they let me out. I couldn't go back to where I was, not physically or mentally. As Uncle Amir always said, Palestine is a whole different experience, people change there, and I did, but not very quickly. It took me a month of staying at home, being away from everything, in order to go back to my normal state of mind and to try to live with the feeling of guilt and weakness. I still don't believe that I fully recovered from that experience; in fact, I don't think anybody should ever recover from it, we have to remember it to have a bigger reason to fight back.

They thought the moment I left, I wouldn't be back there, but they were wrong. Palestine became my second home, I couldn't even stand to be away from it for long.

Every story became mine, there wasn't a special case or a social case going on in the world that I was not involved in. The refugees became my family, the orphans became my children and the weak became my friends. We didn't fight for money, power or popularity... we fought for shelter, food, water and dignity.

People criticised me for only standing up for the Arab people. Well, I didn't choose who to stand up for and favoured the ones that had the same religion or colour as me. No, that wasn't the truth. I stood up for those who deserved to be protected, I stood up for those who deserved a better life, I stood up for those who came knocking on my door, begging for help, because they had no other to turn to. I believe that I fought and am still fighting for every gender, colour and nationality. I am not fighting for a particular race, I am fighting for the human race. People are not aware of this, because I simply don't like to speak much about what I do. I only spoke when it was necessary, because there were and are things that people should hear about, they shouldn't be kept in the dark.

Have you ever been asked this question before: "Are you happy?" I think a lot of us have been asked this question, maybe even multiple times, but how many times were you actually able to answer it?

For me, earlier the answer was as clear as the blue sky... "No, I am not happy, I am very sad, I am depressed, I am swimming in the ocean of darkness without a way out. I don't see or feel this happiness you are talking about. What is this happiness? Do you want me to feel happiness when my father is deep in his grave, when my brother was murdered by cold hearts? When my loved one was shot by his own family? There is no happiness in this world, there is only normal and sad." That was the giving answer. In fact, even before all of this happened, I wasn't happy, I was walking a path, thinking it will end up by me being happy, but I reached a point where I kept thinking that passion I held destroyed me and every one I cared about, so I always said, "Sir, I refuse to give you a different answer, my answer will remain the same for centuries and centuries to come, I will carry it with me to my grave."

Thinking how I was so buried in the darkness, it was normal for me to give such an answer, but it did change... when I reunited with my mother, it became 'no answer'. I couldn't give an answer, I didn't know, I couldn't identify the feelings inside of me. I was better or glad, because I found my mum, but no, I couldn't call it happiness. The feeling wasn't something to be named or explained.

Now, I'll gladly answer that... I am happy.

Happiness doesn't mean always living above the clouds... *la vie en rose*, as they call it. Happiness can be found even in the smallest of things and in the darkest of placesas Albus Dumbledore said in Harry Potter, *"Happiness can be found, even in the darkest of times, if one only remembers to turn on the light."* I am happy, because I am pursuing the dreams I dreamt of; I am happy, because sometimes I make someone smile; I am happy, because sometimes I can be of help, sometimes I can change someone's state from good to better... I am happy because I am true to myself and to the people around me. I am happy, because despite all the things that happened to me, I am able to smile back and love again. And above all, I am happy, because despite the millions offered and the countless threats, I didn't change, nor accepted any of their offers, because I had a case, I have a case... I am not here to win power or collect money. I am here to win hearts, to help who deserves to be helped. I am here because I have a mission to do, and until the day I die, I'll keep fighting for it.

The words you read above were a part of one of my favourite speeches that I ever delivered.

I have delivered many speeches along the way, but this one in particular was special. The speech was delivered at the UNICEF.

Of course, I wouldn't hurt your heads with the full speech which by the way I don't even remember, because it was a made-at-the-moment speech, but there were things I said that I do remember.

"There are things you have in life that are taken for granted. Like leaving for work peacefully in the morning, kissing your children goodbye, sleeping soundly at night, going out on the weekend, watching a film in the cinema, enjoying a walk in the park... All of these are normal things for every citizen, but why does it feel like a faraway dream for us? I dream about sitting in the living room with my family watching the TV, or even eating dinner together. Our children dream about going to the school and learning new things everyday. Let me tell you something, they don't even aspire being something when you ask them, they don't know what it is like to dream, to want to become someone or own something... they don't even own their country. Why would you expect them to dream so far ahead, when they are not even allowed to travel from a government to the other within the boundaries of their country? Let me give you an example, there are people called Palestinians, they live in a place called Gaza. I am sure you all are very familiar with the biggest open-air prison in the world. People there not only children but adults as well don't even know what Al-Quds looks like, they have only seen it in the photos. They can't go out of there, they have relatives they never met.

I am sure there are people in here today who heard such words: Why did you leave your country? Why did you come here? To take ours? Aren't you ashamed of eating our food and using our resources? Well, you weren't very ashamed when you stole ours. We are here because you stole ours. These are the answers that I always give and somehow it manages every time to piss someone so bad, I don't know why.

We are human, we are not your slaves, God didn't make us to serve you or entertain you, and we have the same rights... why are we treated like inferiors? We are in a whole different world right now, we are in the future, these things are supposed to be taught only in the history classes, but no, now we still get bullied, treated badly, get killed for being black, brown, Muslim, Asians... As long as you are not white, you don't deserve to be treated equally, you don't deserve to be a human.

Developed countries always take the lead when it comes to playing the rule. They act like they care; they are such an angel trying to help poor little other countries. Well, excuse us for not seeing the help you are providing. The only thing I see and it's pretty clear to me, is that you are trying to get rid of us, with one way or another, announced or unannounced.

I think we do have differences when it comes to defining help; your definition is very different than ours. So, thank you for all your effort, time and money, but please, stop helping us. We will be fine on our own.

Do you think we like the fact that we are far away from our countries, far away from our home, trying to fit in here while being undesired and unwanted? We didn't and we still don't have the choice, so it's either to die or to leave.

We are not cowards for leaving, we are trying to keep our legacy on by saving our kids and making them remember every single inch of home.

We are not a runaways, we are not running away to forget

or surrender, we are running away to survive and revive.

We are the hope and the only hope for our countries... *we do not forget neither forgive.* We will take back the stolen souls and the vanished laughter.

Every human standing or watching here today is responsible for the killed women, children and men.

I repeat it again and again... we will not forgive nor forget, and we have hope that every stolen land will be returned, that every captivated soul will be freed.

And when that day comes, I'll be standing in front, crying tears of happiness.

You are dreaming of reaching the moon, building a life on Mars, discovering other galaxies and we are dreaming of praying in 'Al Aqsa Mosque' and visiting 'Halab'.

I see your laughing faces pointing at me and telling me what a ridiculous dream you have, but I hit back and say it's not ridiculous, it's our stolen dream and we will take it back.

We will be freed from your slavery, we will be responsible for our fate again.

Live today as much as you can while you are still in power, 'cause tomorrow will come, and we will take the flame back again... not to fire back, but only to light your way to hell.

I remember leaving immediately after saying those words. That night, every single person I knew and even the ones I didn't know called me. Some said I was a hero, others said, "You are done, your career is over."

Well, to be honest, I didn't care about my career or my image. I felt like a hero, I was happy, I felt a strange strength inside of me. I was burning with power and that's the case for all the likes of me, so I didn't care about my death or life because there will be another Ayat fighting as much as I do and maybe even more. I am not one of a kind, I am a piece of a bigger and stronger puzzle.

We all are here to fight to take back what they took from us. I wasn't scared, I was proud and more importantly, my people were proud of me.

At the end, the only think I want to say is that we are surviving and we will keep on surviving till the last breath, and we say it again and again... *we do not forget neither forgive.*

I don't need this to be a top seller or to bring me fame and money. This is the story of us, because someone needs to put it out there, to tell the untold stories, to show people what is happening behind the scenes. They saw the picture of my brother on the beach, but they didn't know the story behind it.

They need to know that family exists, that love exists, they need to know that we were once living just like they did and one day, everything turned upside down.

This is not only a history telling of our terrible memories, but this is a lesson for every single person in this world, for every single soul that doesn't appreciate family, love, and relationships. For those who don't thank God for the little obvious things in their life.

Life is full of surprises, we need to be thankful for everything in it, even the smile of your next-door neighbour because one day you'll miss that too.

Love as much as you can, smile as much as you can and live as much as you can.

I was once standing at the edge of the cliff, ready to jump, thinking that no one will be there to stop me.

Now I can feel a lot of hands clinging to me, stopping me from falling. Hang in there; one day, the light will shine on your dark road again.